FLAVORS
of
SLOVENIA

THE HIPPOCRENE COOKBOOK LIBRARY

AFGHAN FOOD & COOKERY
ALPS, CUISINES OF THE
APROVECHO: A MEXICAN-AMERICAN
    BORDER COOKBOOK
ARGENTINA COOKS!, EXP. ED.
AUSTRIAN CUISINE, BEST OF, EXP. ED.
BOLIVIAN KITCHEN, MY MOTHER'S
BRAZIL: A CULINARY JOURNEY
BURMA, FLAVORS OF
CAJUN CUISINE, STIR THE POT:
    THE HISTORY OF
CAJUN WOMEN, COOKING WITH
CALABRIA, CUCINA DI
CAUCASUS MOUNTAINS, CUISINES OF THE
CHILE, TASTING
COLOMBIAN COOKING, SECRETS OF
CROATIAN COOKING, BEST OF, EXP. ED.
CZECH COOKING, BEST OF, EXP. ED.
DANUBE, ALL ALONG THE, EXP. ED.
EGYPTIAN COOKING
ESTONIAN TASTES AND TRADITIONS
FILIPINO FOOD, FINE
FINNISH COOKING, BEST OF
FRENCH CARIBBEAN CUISINE
FRENCH FASHION, COOKING IN THE
    (Bilingual)
GERMANY, SPOONFULS OF
GREEK COOKING, REGIONAL
GREEK CUISINE, THE BEST OF, EXP. ED.
GYPSY FEAST
HAITI, TASTE OF
HAVANA COOKBOOK, OLD (Bilingual)
HUNGARIAN COOKBOOK, EXP. ED.
ICELANDIC FOOD & COOKERY
INDIA, FLAVORFUL
INDIAN SPICE KITCHEN, THE, EXP. ED.
INTERNATIONAL DICTIONARY OF
    GASTRONOMY
IRISH-STYLE, FEASTING GALORE
ITALIAN CUISINE, TREASURY OF (Bilingual)
JAPANESE HOME COOKING
JEWISH-IRAQI CUISINE, MAMA NAZIMA'S
KOREAN CUISINE, BEST OF
LAOTIAN COOKING, SIMPLE
LATVIA, TASTE OF
LIGURIAN KITCHEN
LITHUANIAN COOKING, ART OF
MACAU, TASTE OF
MALTA, TASTE OF, EXP. ED.

MEXICAN CULINARY TREASURES
MIDDLE EASTERN KITCHEN, THE
NEPAL, TASTE OF
NEW HAMPSHIRE: FROM FARM TO KITCHEN
NEW JERSEY COOKBOOK, FARMS AND FOODS
    OF THE GARDEN STATE:
NORWAY, TASTES AND TALES OF
OHIO, FARMS AND FOODS OF
PERSIAN COOKING, ART OF
PIED NOIR COOKBOOK: FRENCH SEPHARDIC
    CUISINE
PIEMONTESE, CUCINA: COOKING FROM
    ITALY'S PIEDMONT
POLAND'S GOURMET CUISINE
POLISH COOKING, BEST OF, EXP. ED.
POLISH COUNTRY KITCHEN COOKBOOK
POLISH CUISINE, TREASURY OF (Bilingual)
POLISH HERITAGE COOKERY, ILL. ED.
POLISH HOLIDAY COOKERY
POLISH TRADITIONS, OLD
PORTUGUESE ENCOUNTERS, CUISINES OF
PYRENEES, TASTES OF
QUEBEC, TASTE OF
RHINE, ALL ALONG THE
ROMANIA, TASTE OF, EXP. ED.
RUSSIAN COOKING, BEST OF, EXP. ED.
SCOTLAND, TRADITIONAL FOOD FROM
SCOTTISH-IRISH PUB AND HEARTH COOKBOOK
SEPHARDIC ISRAELI CUISINE
SICILIAN FEASTS
SLOVENIA, FLAVORS OF
SMORGASBORD COOKING, BEST OF
SOUTH AMERICAN COOKERY
SOUTH INDIAN COOKING, HEALTHY
SPANISH FAMILY COOKBOOK, REV. ED.
SRI LANKA, EXOTIC TASTES OF
SWEDISH KITCHEN, A
TAIWANESE CUISINE, BEST OF
THAI CUISINE, BEST OF REGIONAL
TRINIDAD AND TOBAGO, SWEET HANDS:
    ISLAND COOKING FROM
TURKISH CUISINE, TASTE OF
TUSCAN KITCHEN, TASTES FROM A
UKRAINIAN CUISINE, BEST OF, EXP. ED.
UZBEK COOKING, ART OF
VIETNAMESE KITCHEN, A
WALES, GOOD FOOD FROM
WARSAW COOKBOOK, OLD

FLAVORS

of

SLOVENIA

FOOD *and* WINE *from* CENTRAL EUROPE'S HIDDEN GEM

Heike Milhench

HIPPOCRENE BOOKS, INC.
NEW YORK

Copyright © 2007 by Heike Milhench.

Jacket and book design by Pooja Pottenkulam.
Photography by Heike Milhench.

For more information, address:

HIPPOCRENE BOOKS, INC.
171 Madison Avenue
New York, NY 10016
www.hippocrenebooks.com

Library of Congress Cataloging-in-Publication Data

Milhench, Heike.
    Flavors of Slovenia / Heike Milhench.
        p. cm.
    Includes bibliographical references and index.

    ISBN-13: 978-0-7818-1170-5
    ISBN-10: 0-7818-1170-8

        1. Cookery, Slovenian. 2. Cookery—Slovenia. I. Title.

TX723.5.S6M44 2007
641.594973—dc22   2007016389

Printed in the United States of America.

For my father

CONTENTS

SIDEBARS

As we steamed out of the station, the [German] manufacturer said with a rolling laugh, "Well, we'll have no more good food till we're back here again. The food in Yugoslavia is terrible." "Ach, so we have heard," wailed the business man's wife… "There is nothing good at all, is there?" This seemed to me extremely funny, for food in Yugoslavia has a Slav superbness. They cook lamb and sucking-pig as well as anywhere in the world, have a lot of freshwater fish and broil it straight out of the streams, use their vegetables young enough, have many dark and rich romantic soups, and understand that seasoning should be pungent rather than hot. I said, "You needn't worry at all. Yugoslavian food is very good."

– Rebecca West, *Black Lamb and Grey Falcon: A Journey through Yugoslavia, 1942*

ACKNOWLEDGMENTS

First and foremost, I would like to heartily thank all of my Slovenian friends who helped me to collect recipes and advice for this book. Many thanks to Polde Mavec, Dušan Furar, Marina Kristanc, and, of course, Cveto Pogačar from the Grand Hotel Toplice. Thanks also to Janez Fajfar from Vila Bled, and to Arno Pucher from Gostilna pri Planincu, and to Leo Ličof from Okarina. Many thanks also to Dietmar from Penzion Mayer.

I would also like to thank Gregor Šuc from the Slovenian Embassy in Washington. Many thanks also to my friends and family who have helped and supported me along the way. Especially to Jens and Jeanette, my travel companions; Jolene, the Hungarian expert; Maja, the Croatian expert; John O'Brien, who introduced me to Bled; Elke; Mom; Tatjana; and, of course, to Siri Lise Doub, for her encouragement.

I will always be grateful to my father for passing his love of travel on to me.

INTRODUCTION

Slovenia is a beautiful land in Central Europe, tucked between the foothills of the Alps, the coast of the Adriatic Sea, and the beginning of the Panonian plains to the East. A country of almost 2 million people, Slovenia has survived centuries of domination by other powers, such as the Austro-Hungarian Empire. Today, it is an independent country, and one of the more recent members of the European Union. The country's natural beauty, the warmth of its people, and the richness and diversity of its culture make it a wonderful place to visit and explore.

One of the greatest attributes of Slovenian cuisine is its use of local and fresh ingredients. In the early summer, for example, one will see many asparagus dishes on local menus; in the fall, pumpkin soup and venison; in the spring, dandelion salad. The regional dishes are strongly influenced by the surrounding geography, be it the mountainous region of Gorenjska in the northwest, or the seaside region of Primorska on the Adriatic Coast. Local tastes also mirror the cultures of neighboring countries. For example, the northeast region of Prekmurje prefers spicy soups and stews, typical of Hungarian cuisine, whereas the Koroška region along the border of Austria enjoys foods with more of an Austrian or Germanic influence. The Primorska region, along the western border of Slovenia, shows its appreciation of Italian cuisine.

Although this book includes many traditional recipes, such as Brown Soup and Strudel, there are also some modern twists on old favorites, such as Zucchini Fritters. My selections reflect the Slovenia of today. Many Slovenian restaurants feature traditional dishes; however, creative gourmet chefs also like to make their mark on the menu. For example, there are wonderful new restaurants in Ljubljana, as well as in the mountains, which feature "Slovenian Slow Food" menus. These contrast with the Slovenian version of "fast food," *čevapčiči*, a spiced meat served on the streets of Ljubljana, that has roots in the cuisine of the southern Balkans.

Dining in Slovenia is pleasantly accompanied by the local wines, beers, and other beverages. The country has a long history of wine production, and hundreds of small vineyards produce high-quality wines. Depending on which region you are in, you will drink one of three local beers brewed from the well-known Štajerska hops: Union Pivo brewed in Ljubljana; Laško Pivo from Laško; or beer from the smaller Gambrinus brewery in Maribor. Traditional brandies, such as blueberry, pear, and walnut, are produced on farms, in monasteries, or in kitchens. Slovenians also enjoy the local cola, juices, and iced tea, proudly bottled at home.

When you go to Slovenia, you will be amazed by how much there is to do within its modest borders. There is skiing, golf, hiking and rock climbing, sailing, fishing, and whitewater rafting. You can visit the Lipizzaner horses, thermal baths, wine vineyards, and crystal factories, as well as a World War I museum, beautiful medieval castles, and art nouveau architecture. Everywhere you go, you will find wonderful restaurants, pubs, and cafés, and will be greeted by open and friendly Slovenians, very interested to know where you came from and how you came to visit Slovenia. Enjoy the recipes and stories within this book–I hope they will inspire you to make the trip!

Dober tek! (Bon appétit!)

A TOAST Zdravljica

1847

Anew the vines have fruited
And borne us, my good friends, sweet wine
To charge our blood diluted,
To clear our heart, our eye define,
To suppress
All distress
And waken hope in saddened breast.

Now whom for our first tipple
Shall we, glad brothers, toast in song?
Our land, us Slovene people
May God endow with lifetime long,
Where'er found,
Brothers bound
As sons to mother much renowned!

May our home skies wage warfare,
With thunder strike the enemy!
Henceforth, as were our forebears',
May Slovenes' homes be truly free;
Let their hands
Iron bands
Constrict, who still oppress our lands!

May unity, joy, blessing
Return, may we be reconciled!
And, brotherhood professing,
Close linked be Slava's every child,
That again
We may reign
And honour, riches now again!

God grant you, Slovene women,
Long life, O noblest flowers fair!
To our own kindred maiden
The like is not found anywhere;
From you be
Progeny
To terrify the enemy!

Young men, our future's promise,
Our hope, we raise a toast to you!
Your love for home and birthplace
May no one poison, none undo!
In the end
You will tend
The hour to boldly it defend!

Let's drink that every nation
Will live to see that bright day's birth
When 'neath the sun's rotation
Dissent is banished from the earth,
All will be
Kinfolk free
With neighbors none in enmity.

And last, my friends, come hither,
Let's raise unto ourselves a toast!
For we have come together,
The common good we cherish most.
God, we praise,
Grant us days
In plenty, for our virtuous way!

– France Prešeren, Slovenian national poet.
Translated by Tom Priestly and
Henry Cooper

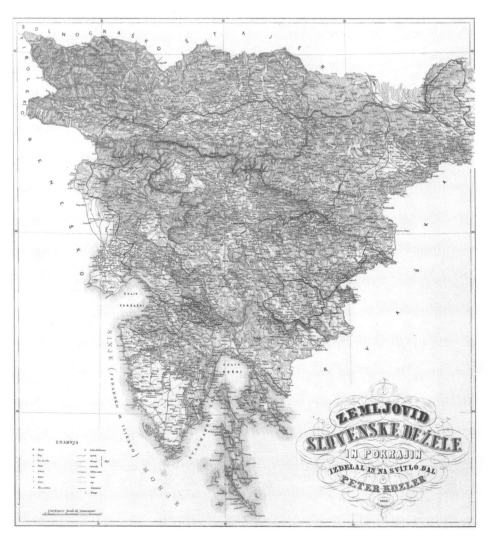

Map of Slovenian lands stretching from the island of Cres in the south
(now Croatia) to Tirol in the north (now Austria), 1853.

Appetizers

Čas setve še ni čas žetve.
The time to sow is not the time to reap.

– Slovenian proverb

Wild Mushroom Strudel Divji Gobji Zavitek

In Slovenia, a favorite pastime in the fall is to collect wild mushrooms from the local forests. Families and friends gather, carrying picnic lunches, and make a day of walking through the woods, selecting mushrooms, and resting with homemade sandwiches and a bottle of wine. The mushrooms are brought home and used in many delicious recipes, such as this tasty appetizer.

Serves 6 as an appetizer; 3 as a main meal

6 tablespoons (¾ stick) butter
12 ounces mushrooms (button, or a combination of portobello, shiitake, or oyster), cleaned and sliced
1 egg
1 cup cream
1 tablespoon Dijon mustard
2 slices white bread (sourdough adds a nice flavor), crusts removed, cubed
1 clove garlic, minced
Freshly ground pepper
3 sheets phyllo dough

1. Preheat oven to 350°F.
2. Butter a baking sheet with 1 tablespoon of butter.
3. Melt 3 tablespoons of butter in a saucepan. Add the mushrooms and sauté for 12 to 15 minutes, or until the mushrooms are tender and all the liquid has evaporated. Cool.
4. In a bowl, beat together the egg, cream and mustard.
5. Once the mushrooms have cooled, mix together the mushrooms, bread cubes, garlic, pepper to taste, and cream mixture.
6. Melt the remaining 2 tablespoons of butter.
7. Roll out one of the phyllo sheets and brush with melted butter. Spread ⅓ of the mushroom mixture on the sheet, leaving a 2 to 3-inch margin on each side of the sheet. Fold up the left and the right sides of the pastry over the mixture, then roll the pastry into a strudel, sealing the end of the dough with a dab of melted butter. Repeat the above with the remaining phyllo and mushroom mixture.
8. Place the strudels on the prepared baking sheet and bake for 25 minutes, or until browned.
9. Slice the strudel into small pieces to serve as a salty snack with a light red wine, such as a *Cviček*, or beer. Or serve as an hors d'oeuvre, or as a meal with a salad.

Hearty Potato Pancake Friko

An English journalist recently reported for The Guardian *while visiting Slovenia, calling this hearty and tasty dish—originating from the Primorska (coastal) region—both "gob-smacking" and "rib-sticking." With a little bit of creativity, simple ingredients can be used to make a savory and tasty dish.* Friko *is made with leftover potatoes, eggs, and cheese, ingredients often found in your cupboard on a Sunday evening. Friko makes a hearty breakfast, a tasty appetizer, or light evening supper with a salad and a glass of red wine, such as a Teran.*

Serves 4 as an appetizer; 2 as a main meal

2 to 3 tablespoons bacon fat, lard, or butter
2 medium potatoes (about 1 pound), peeled and sliced thinly
½ teaspoon salt
Freshly ground pepper
4 eggs
½ pound any kind of hard cheese, grated (approximately 1 cup)
Grated cheese, chives, or parsley, for garnish (optional)

1. Melt the fat in a medium skillet over medium heat.
2. Place the potato slices evenly in the pan. Sprinkle with salt and pepper. Fry the potatoes on both sides until they are tender on the inside and slightly browned on the outside (10 to 15 minutes each side).
3. Beat the eggs in a small bowl.
4. Add the grated cheese to the eggs.
5. Pour the egg and cheese mixture into the pan over the cooked potatoes.
6. Cook until the eggs are browned on the bottom (5 to 10 minutes).
7. Flip the friko and brown on the other side, cooking for another 4 to 5 minutes.
8. Transfer the browned friko to a serving dish.
9. Garnish to taste with grated cheese, freshly ground pepper, or chopped chives or parsley. Serve with sour cream, if you wish.

Olive Tapenade Olivni Namaz

Also found in Provence and Italy, this pungent spread is made in Slovenia with olives that grow along the Adriatic Coast. Green or black olives may be used in this recipe. There are many variations, all of them showing the Dalmatian influence on some favorite Slovenian recipes. For example, you may add a clove of garlic, chopped fresh parsley, fresh thyme, or capers to your tapenade, to suit your taste. The tapenade goes well with crackers, crudites, bread, fish, meat, or pasta. Enjoy with a cold glass of white wine, such as a Renski Rizling or a Beli Pinot.

Makes 2 cups

1 cup oil-cured black or
  green olives, pitted and
  drained
4 to 6 oil-packed anchovy
  fillets, drained
2 teaspoons powdered
  mustard
Freshly ground black
  pepper
1 teaspoon dried thyme
2 tablespoons freshly
  squeezed lemon juice,
  strained
½ cup extra-virgin olive oil

1. Combine all of the ingredients, except for the olive oil, in a food processor. Process until the ingredients form a paste.
2. Scrape the sides of the bowl. Process again, slowly adding the olive oil to the mixture. Process until the mixture is creamy. Season to taste.
3. Refrigerate, covered, until ready to use.

Omelet in Wine Vinska Omleta

This dish, considered a delicacy in peasant homes, was often served to new mothers to provide them with nourishment and strength. Although traditionally reserved for special occasions, today this dish makes a great light supper with fresh bread and a salad. The more wine you add at the end, the more sauce you will have to soak your bread in!

Serves 1

2 eggs
1 tablespoon grated
   Parmesan cheese
Salt and freshly ground
   pepper
2 tablespoons butter
½ cup white wine

1. Beat the eggs in a bowl until they are frothy. Add the Parmesan cheese and salt and pepper to taste.
2. Melt the butter in an omelet pan or small skillet with a lid, over medium heat.
3. Once the butter is melted, add the egg mixture to the pan. Cook at medium heat for 3 to 4 minutes, or until the egg mixture is browned on one side. Flip the omelet and cook for 2 to 3 minutes more, or until browned on the other side.
4. Add the white wine to the pan and cover. Cook covered for about 1 minute.
5. Serve immediately.

Zucchini Fritters Ocvrt Jajčevec

These fritters show the northern Italian influence on Slovenian cuisine. They make an excellent appetizer, or can also be served as a vegetable side dish with fish or meat. Using baby zucchini makes this hot appetizer especially tender and delicious.

Makes 24 small fritters; 12 medium fritters

1 pound zucchini
  (2 or 3 medium),
  trimmed and grated
¼ cup all-purpose flour
¼ cup Parmesan cheese,
  grated
1 egg, slightly beaten
¼ teaspoon nutmeg
¼ teaspoon salt
Freshly ground pepper
Olive oil, for frying

Optional garnishes:
  Sour cream
  Parmesan cheese, grated
  Chopped fresh parsley
    or basil

1. Place the grated zucchini in a large bowl. Add the flour, Parmesan cheese, egg, nutmeg, salt and pepper. Stir until you have formed a thick batter. Add an additional tablespoon or two of flour if necessary to get the right consistency.
2. Pour olive oil into a large heavy-bottomed skillet until the oil is ½ inch deep. Heat over medium heat until the oil sizzles when water is sprinkled in the pan.
3. Place large spoonfuls of batter into the hot oil, and flatten them with a spatula, not letting the fritters touch. Cook for 5 to 8 minutes, or until the fritters are browned on one side. Then flip them over, and cook them for 3 to 5 minutes, or until they are browned on the other side. When the fritters are browned evenly on both sides, remove them from the pan, and drain on paper towels. Repeat with the remaining batter.
4. Serve immediately; they will get soggy if you try to keep them warm. Serve with sour cream, additional grated Parmesan cheese, fresh herbs, or plain, as you wish.

Frittata with Prosciutto Frtalja s Pršutom

This is another example of the Italian influence on Slovenian food. Made with eggs, cheese, and a variety of fillings, the frittata is the Italian version of an omelet. Shown here with two variations, frtalja *can be served as an appetizer, or for breakfast, lunch, or a light supper with a salad or fresh fruit. Prosciutto,* pršut, *salted and air-dried ham, is a common delicacy all over the Adriatic Coast. Often it is aired in the lofts of pig farmers' barns throughout the winter, which allows mountain breezes to give it its natural flavor. Its salty and fragrant taste is especially enjoyed in the spring. Prosciutto adds nice flavor to this frittata, and complements the Parmesan cheese. (For a recipe for Pršut, see page 38; it can also be bought in many larger American supermarkets and delis.)*

Serves 2

Olive oil
4 slices prosciutto,
  cut into small pieces
½ cup grated Parmesan
  cheese
4 eggs
½ cup milk
½ teaspoon salt
⅓ cup chopped fresh
  herbs, such as parsley,
  basil, or oregano
Freshly ground pepper

1. Preheat the oven to 400°F.

2. Coat the bottom of an 8-inch pie plate or round baking dish with olive oil.

3. Spread the prosciutto evenly on the bottom of the baking dish. Sprinkle the Parmesan cheese evenly on top of the prosciutto.

4. Beat the eggs in a small bowl. Blend in the milk. Add the salt and chopped herbs.

5. Pour the egg mixture over the top of the cheese and prosciutto. Season to taste with freshly ground pepper.

6. Bake for approximately 20 minutes until slightly browned on top and the eggs have puffed up. Make sure that the eggs are cooked thoroughly, but do not overcook.

Frittata with Fresh Herbs Zeliščna Frtalja

This version of a frittata features delicious herbs.

Serves 2

Olive oil
**½ cup finely chopped,
   mixed fresh herbs such as
   basil, parsley, thyme,
   marjoram, oregano,
   or sage**
4 eggs
½ cup milk
½ teaspoon salt
Freshly ground pepper

1. Preheat the oven to 400°F.
2. Coat the bottom of an 8-inch pie plate or round baking dish with olive oil. Sprinkle the fresh herbs on the bottom of the baking dish.
3. Beat the eggs in a small bowl. Blend in the milk. Add the salt.
4. Pour the egg mixture over the herbs. Season to taste with freshly ground pepper.
5. Bake for approximately 20 minutes until the frittata is slightly browned on top and the eggs have puffed up. Make sure that the eggs are cooked thoroughly, but do not overcook.

Fried Olives Ocvrte Olive

Fried olives are a tasty treat with a cocktail or a glass of wine. In Slovenia and in northern Italy, they are often served in bars in place of peanuts or with other snacks. At the Movia Vineyard in Brda, fried olives are served during wine tastings to clear the palate.

Makes 36 small or 24 medium fried olives

1 egg
½ cup cornmeal
¼ teaspoon salt
Olive oil, for frying
2½ ounces olives (approximately 36 small or 24 medium), pitted, rinsed, and patted dry

1. Beat the egg in a shallow bowl with a teaspoon of water.

2. Pour the cornmeal into another shallow bowl. Mix in the salt.

3. Coat the bottom of a skillet with ¼-inch layer of olive oil. Heat the oil on medium heat for 4 to 5 minutes.

4. One by one, take each olive and roll in the egg mixture, then in the cornmeal mixture, until the olive is covered in cornmeal.

5. Fry each olive in the oil for 5 to 8 minutes, or until lightly browned on all sides. With a spatula, roll the olives around periodically so that they brown evenly.

6. Remove from the pan and dry on a paper towel. Serve immediately.

Fried Small Fish 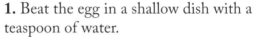 Pečene Sardele

Although Slovenian fishermen love to brag about the large fish that they capture, oftentimes the first fish prepared after a catch are the smaller fish, creating a fresh snack or appetizer upon arrival in port. Fried small fish make a salty, tasty snack with a beer or a glass of coastal white wine. A variety of smaller fish, such as smelts, mackerel, or sardines, can be used. Smaller fish can be rolled in flour, fried until crispy, and eaten whole. Larger fish should be cleaned and their head and backbone removed before cooking.

Serves 4 as an appetizer

1 egg
1 cup all-purpose flour
½ teaspoon salt
Freshly ground pepper
Olive oil, for frying
½ pound fresh sardines
** or smelts**
Lemon wedges

1. Beat the egg in a shallow dish with a teaspoon of water.
2. Place flour in a second shallow bowl. Mix in the salt and pepper.
3. Coat the bottom of a skillet with ¼-inch layer of olive oil. Heat on medium heat until the oil starts to sputter.
4. Roll each fish in the egg mixture, then in the flour mixture, until covered in flour.
5. Fry the fish for 3 to 4 minutes, or until they are browned on one side, then flip over and cook 3 to 4 minutes on the other side, or until browned.
6. Remove from the pan and dry on a paper towel.
7. Sprinkle with freshly squeezed lemon juice and serve immediately.

Wild Mushrooms Cooked in Butter and Garlic Divji Gobji Zavitek z Maslom in Česnom

In the fall in Slovenia, one can enjoy a variety of fresh wild mushrooms in many dishes. Sometimes the simplest dishes are the tastiest, as this wonderful appetizer shows. A favorite at the Okarina Restaurant in Bled, the earthy mushrooms sautéed in garlic go well with a heavy red wine, such as a Merlot. Outside Slovenia, local fresh wild mushrooms are available at farmers' markets in the fall. During the rest of the year, cultivated exotic mushrooms can be mixed with standard mushrooms to make this dish affordable and delicious.

Serves 2 as an appetizer

4 tablespoons (½ stick) butter
1 pound fresh mushrooms (button or a combination of portobello, shiitake, or oyster), washed thoroughly and cut into thick slices
¼ cup heavy cream
2 cloves garlic, minced
2 tablespoons chopped fresh parsley
½ teaspoon salt
Freshly ground pepper

1. In a skillet, melt the butter over medium heat.
2. Add the mushrooms to the pan. Cook, stirring over medium heat, for 15 to 20 minutes, or until most of the liquid has evaporated from the pan. Remove from the heat.
3. Add the cream, garlic, and parsley, and toss. Season to taste with salt and pepper.
4. Serve immediately with fresh bread and a heavy red wine.

Ravno sredi mojga srca
Ena rožica cveti,
Če ne boš jo zalivala,
Se zagvišno posuši.

**Traditional Slovenian couple painted on a postcard by
Maksim Gaspari.**

Portobello Mushrooms with Garlic and Gorgonzola Cheese

Šampijoni z Česnom in Gorgonzolevo Omako

Another fall dish, this is a favorite appetizer at the Bled Golf and Country Club restaurant. After a round of eighteen holes on this beautiful mountainous course, one can sit on the outdoor terrace looking over the Julian Alps and enjoy this tasty dish with a cold beer brewed at the local Union Brewery.

Serves 2 as an appetizer

3 tablespoons butter

6 portobello mushrooms, cleaned, and cut into ¼-inch slices

¼ cup Gorgonzola cheese, crumbled (approximately 2 ounces)

2 small cloves garlic, minced

Salt and freshly ground pepper

Fresh parsley, washed, dried, and chopped (optional)

1. Melt the butter in a skillet with a lid.

2. Add the mushrooms to the pan. Cook, stirring over medium heat for 5 to 6 minutes, or until slightly browned on one side. Then flip the mushrooms and cook, stirring for 4 to 5 minutes, or until slightly browned on the other side.

3. When the mushrooms are browned evenly on both sides, and most of the moisture has evaporated, reduce the heat to low.

4. Sprinkle the mushrooms evenly with the Gorgonzola cheese and the minced garlic. Cover the pan for 2 minutes. When the cheese has melted slightly, remove the pan from the heat. Season with salt and freshly ground pepper. Sprinkle with parsley, if desired.

5. Transfer the mushrooms to a plate. Serve immediately with fresh bread.

Chicken Livers with Mushrooms

Pražena Kurja Jetrca z Gobicami

Sunday afternoon lunch in Slovenia is a family affair that can last for hours. Several courses are served, sometimes accompanied by several bottles of wine. Especially during the winter months, the chance to sit together in a warm and cozy atmosphere to catch up on the week's events is appreciated by all. This hearty, warm appetizer can often kick off such a meal. The chicken livers can be served over polenta or toast, or with fresh bread. A strong red wine is recommended.

Serves 4 as an appetizer

3 tablespoons butter
3 tablespoons minced
  scallions or shallots
⅓ pound mushrooms
  (wild or cultivated),
  cleaned and sliced
1 tablespoon olive oil
1 pound chicken livers,
  rinsed, patted dry, and
  trimmed
¼ teaspoon salt
Freshly ground black
  pepper
1½ tablespoons lemon
  juice
½ cup cream (optional)
1 tablespoon minced fresh
  parsley

1. Melt the butter in a large skillet. Add the shallots or scallions and cook over medium heat for 6 to 8 minutes, or until softened.
2. Add the mushrooms. Cook, stirring until the mushrooms are golden brown. Remove the mushrooms and shallots from the pan and set aside.
3. Warm the olive oil in the pan. When the oil is hot enough so that it sizzles when water is sprinkled in the pan, add the livers to the pan. Sear the livers over medium heat for 8 to 10 minutes, or until golden brown on all sides. Do not overcook.
4. Return the mushrooms and shallots to the pan. Season with salt and pepper to taste. Add the lemon juice.
5. Add the cream, if desired. Add the parsley and stir. Let the mixture cook for 1 to 2 minutes, until the livers have heated through. (Do not let the sauce boil.)
6. Serve with toast, polenta or fresh bread.

Asparagus with Prosciutto Beluši s Šunko

During the early summer, when asparagus, green or white, is fresh and abundant from local farms, Slovenians eat it as if it is going out of style (or out of season!). Unlike in the United States, where large supermarkets provide all kinds of imported fruits and vegetables throughout the year, Slovenians eat what is fresh and in season from local farms and fields. And so, all over Slovenia, mid-June menus feature an array of asparagus recipes. This cold appetizer is one of the many asparagus dishes served during these "Days of Asparagus" at the restaurant of Pension Mayer, a small family-run hotel overlooking Lake Bled.

Serves 4 as an appetizer

1 pound asparagus
12 to 14 slices prosciutto
Olive oil
Salt
Freshly ground pepper

1. Soak the asparagus in cold water. To trim, hold the base of a stalk of asparagus with one hand, and place your other hand along the stem a few inches away. Bend the asparagus gently so that the tender part snaps off from the hard stem. Repeat this with each piece of asparagus. Discard the hard ends.
2. Pour ½ to 1 inch of slightly salted water into a large saucepan. Add the asparagus; the asparagus should lie flat in the pan.
3. Place on high heat and cover the pan. Allow the asparagus to steam for 5 to 7 minutes. Do not overcook. They should be tender but firm and not mushy. Drain.
4. Take 3 or 4 stalks of asparagus and wrap them in a slice of prosciutto.
5. Prepare 3 to 4 of these "packages" per serving.
6. Drizzle with olive oil, and season to taste with salt and pepper.

The Pension Mayer in Bled is a family-run restaurant and hotel.

Smoked Trout with Scrambled Eggs Postrv z Mešanimi Jajci

Trout are abundant in the rivers of Slovenia. Freshly grilled trout is on many menus all year round. In this recipe, smoked trout adds a nice flavor to scrambled eggs. The fresh herbs keep it light and fresh.

Serves 4 as an appetizer

6 eggs
2 tablespoons sour cream
¼ teaspoon salt
Freshly ground pepper
3 tablespoons butter
4 smoked trout fillets, cut into thin slices
½ cup chopped fresh herbs such as parsley, chives, or tarragon

1. In a bowl, beat the eggs. Stir in the sour cream, salt and pepper.

2. Melt the butter in a large skillet over medium heat.

3. Add the egg mixture. Cook over medium heat, stirring continuously.

4. As the eggs begin to cook, after 3 to 4 minutes, add the trout.

5. Continue to cook, stirring for another 3 to 4 minutes. As the eggs become firm, add the herbs and stir. The scrambled eggs should be firm, but moist. Do not overcook the eggs by letting them become dry.

6. Remove the eggs from the pan and place on warm plates. Serve with buttered toast.

Baked Encrusted Pig or Veal Lung

Mežerli

This is a hearty, traditional dish made with pig or veal lungs or heart. Like a Scottish haggis, it is an example of a farmer's dish served at harvest time. When an animal is slaughtered, every bit of it is used. The lungs and heart are good sources of protein, vitamins, and minerals. The bread crumbs, sour cream, and marjoram add good flavor. When this dish is done, it develops a rich, golden crust. Serve with a salad and a dry white wine such as a Mariborčan or a Chardonnay.

Serves 5 to 6 as an appetizer, or serves 3 to 4 as a small meal

Salt
2 to 2½ pounds veal or pig's lung, or pig's heart, washed
4 tablespoons fat, lard, or butter
2 medium onions, peeled and chopped
¼ teaspoon marjoram
Freshly ground pepper
2 cups day-old white bread, cubed finely
⅓ cup sour cream
2 eggs, lightly beaten
1 cup milk

1. Wash the lungs or heart. Fill a large saucepan three-quarters full with salted water. Cook the lungs in the salted water over high heat for 1 to 1½ hours, or until they have softened.
2. Remove the lungs from the boiling water, saving some of the water in which they were cooked.
3. Allow the lungs to cool, then chop into small pieces.
4. Preheat the oven to 375°F.
5. In a skillet, melt 3 tablespoons of the fat over medium heat. Add the onions. Cook and stir until the onions are translucent. Add the lung pieces, marjoram and pepper. Cook and stir over medium heat for 4 to 5 minutes. Remove from heat.
6. In a large bowl, mix the bread cubes, sour cream, and beaten eggs. Add ½ cup of the stock used to cook the lungs. Add the lung mixture to the bread. Stir. Add the milk slowly and stir until a loose batter is formed. If the mixture is too thick, add more milk.
7. Grease a baking pan or pie plate with the remaining 1 tablespoon of fat. Add the *mežerli* mixture. Bake for 45 minutes, or until the crust is golden brown.

Baccalà Bakala

Bakala *is a pâté or spread made from dried, salted cod, which is very popular along the Adriatic Coast. It is often served with bread or toast at the beginning of a meal. It is easy to find dried, salted cod in the markets of Slovenia and Croatia. Elsewhere, salt cod can be found in specialty stores or through such catalogs as the Vermont Country Store.*

Serves 6 as an appetizer

2 pounds dried, salted cod, or smoked white fish
2 cups olive oil
1 tablespoon salt

1. If you are using dried cod, soak the cod in water until it becomes soft, then drain.
2. Flake the fish, removing the bones. Place in a bowl.
3. Add the olive oil and salt to the fish. Stir, forming a thick paste.
4. Serve the bakala with freshly toasted bread and white wine.

Cheese Board

Sirova Polšča

Throughout Slovenia, especially in the wine country, a cheese board is often full of tasty salty and savory local treats that complement the local wines. The snacks are also used to clear the palate when tasting wines. Here are some suggestions of what to include in your cheese board.

A variety of hard cheeses including
  Parmesan and sheep's cheese
A variety of olives
Breadsticks
Crackers or cheese crisps
Fresh bread
Fresh fruit, such as grapes or apples
Dried fruit, such as figs
Salted nuts

Bacon Fat or Lard

Svinjska Mast

Another treat that is often served with bread before a meal is bacon fat or lard. Restaurants will frequently save the fat that results from the cooking of ham, bacon, or other fatty meats; it is placed in small pots and chilled. The fat is delicious spread on fresh bread. You can do the same at home when you fry bacon or cook other meats. Reserve the fat, place into decorative pots, and chill. Decorate with fresh, chopped parsley, and serve with fresh bread.

Prosciutto Pršut

Prosciutto is regularly served in parts of Central Europe, especially in the region along the Adriatic Coast. It is a popular appetizer, together with olives, sheep's cheese, and bread. It is also served with asparagus, eggs, fresh figs, or other fruits and vegetables. Prosciutto can easily be found in supermarkets or gourmet stores, but it varies in quality. If you would like to make it yourself, a traditional recipe follows.

Makes 4 to 5 pounds of prosciutto

Garlic cloves from 2 heads of garlic, peeled and crushed
2 to 3 cups salt
3 to 4 tablespoons freshly ground pepper
8 to 10 bay leaves, crushed
10 sprigs fresh rosemary
1 upper leg joint of a one-year-old pig

1. Prepare a mixture of the garlic, salt, pepper, bay leaves and rosemary.

2. Spread the mixture over the meat. Let it sit in a roasting dish for 4 to 5 days, chilled.

3. Place a board or heavy weight, covered in a clean kitchen cloth, over the meat. Let sit for another few days, chilled, allowing the moisture to drain out of the meat.

4. With more of the salt mixture, cover the meat, making sure to tuck curing mixture into the cracks in the meat that have formed.

5. Hang the meat outdoors in an open, airy covered place (such as the attic of a barn) for 11 to 12 months. It is said that the best place for this purpose is along the Adriatic Coast, where the dry, cold winds from the northern mountains (the "bora" winds) blow during the winter.

THE SLOVENIAN SEASHORE: WORTH ITS SALT

Although the Slovenian seashore along the Adriatic Sea is small in comparison to such countries as Italy or Croatia, it has played an important role in Slovenian history and its economy over the years. Used as a port in Roman times, Koper remains a working port, and the surrounding regions produce wonderful white wines. Piran is a beautiful Venetian town that has maintained its medieval character; today it supports a large fishing fleet. Housing a saltworks museum and nature preserve, Sečovlje is the setting of some 2,500 acres of abandoned saltpans, where salt was "mined" from the sea as far back as the thirteenth century. Sea salt has traditionally been considered better than mined salt; with no metallic taste, it dissolves more quickly, and has a stronger flavor. In the nineteenth century, the salt was used at the thermal spa at Portorož to treat rheumatism and other muscular disorders. Portorož became famous late in that century, when Austro-Hungarian officers enjoyed its mud baths.

In the Middle Ages, Sečovlje was a hive of activity, producing precious sea salt in large quantities, which was then sold to Venice and Austria. Now a series of deserted canals, dikes, and pools, the saltpans once housed the families of seasonal workers who collected and transported the salt.

The traditional method of collecting sea salt, employed until thirty-five years ago, is still used today by museum workers who produce 180 tons of salt in Sečovlje every year.

Seawater was channeled into the saltpans through a series of canals. The water was guided into shallow pools, that were lined with a hard, pressed material made with gypsum and microorganisms called petola. The pools were separated by dikes dammed by wooden paddles. Wind-powered pumps, fitted with large sheets as on a windmill, together with the sun and the wind, helped evaporate the water, allowing the salt to crystallize. The dried salt was collected, washed, and loaded onto barges for transport to warehouses along the coast. Oftentimes, the salt was stored on the first floor of the salt workers' houses before it was ready to be shipped.

The salt workers would collect salt only during the summer months, when the sun was shining. Their living quarters were located on the second floor of their houses, which had large windows, allowing the workers to see oncoming rainstorms well in advance, giving them enough time to fetch the collecting salt. Salt workers often returned to their farms in the fall, to tend their crops and animals. These people were referred to as "sitting on two chairs" because they worked two industries in two different seasons.

Today, the saltpans are a peaceful setting. The nature reserve is an amazing place for bird watchers, and the museum is an interesting visit for anyone in the area.

An old postcard depicting the transport of salt from the saltpans at Sečovlje.

Rajši srce brez besed kot besede brez srca.
A heart with no words is better than words with no heart.

– Slovenian Proverb

Tam ostani, kjer pojo; hubobni pesmi nimajo.
Stay where people sing; the mean don't know any songs.

– Slovenian proverb

Soups, Stews, and Hot Pots

It would seem that the Carinthians used up most of their talent on music, leaving little for the kitchen. Indeed, the people of this land have an exceptional ear for music; their dishes, on the other hand, are ascetic, mellow and lyrical, much like the people themselves.

– Matjaž Kmecl, *Slovenian Cookery; Over 100 Classic Dishes*

Brown Soup Goveja Juha

Although this soup may not have the most appetizing name in English, it is a traditional Slovenian beef stock dish. "Soup vegetables" can mean anything from carrots and turnips to an onion. Use what you have or what appeals to you. This can be used as a rich beef stock for the base of other soups, or can be served as is, as a warm appetizer to a winter dinner.

Makes 2 quarts of beef broth

1 tablespoon lard or butter
Soup vegetables,
  for example:
  3 to 4 carrots, peeled and
    sliced
  1 parsley root, cleaned
    and sliced
  1 to 2 medium onions,
    peeled and quartered
  2 to 3 stalks celery
1 garlic clove, peeled
1 bay leaf
3 to 8 peppercorns
1 pound beef, cut into
  chunks (any cut is fine)
¼ pound chicken or beef
  liver, trimmed
½ pound veal, cut into
  chunks (optional)
2 quarts beef broth or
  water

1. Melt the lard in a large saucepan over medium heat.
2. Add the soup vegetables, garlic, bay leaf, peppercorns, beef, liver and veal. Cook, stirring, over medium heat until the meat is browned.
3. Add the beef broth. Cook over low heat for 1 hour.
4. If you like a clear soup, pour the soup through a sieve before serving. Otherwise, serve as is.

Brown Flour or Caraway Seed Soup

Prežganka

Another version of Brown Soup, this soup is flour based. The caraway seeds add an interesting flavor, and the eggs make it hearty. This is a great soup to warm you up on a cold evening. Slovenian mothers sometimes serve this to their sick children.

Makes 2 cups of soup

4 tablespoons (½ stick) butter
¼ cup flour
1 teaspoon caraway seeds
Freshly ground pepper
1 teaspoon salt
4 cups water
2 eggs, slightly beaten
Chopped chervil or parsley, for garnish

1. Melt the butter in a large saucepan over medium heat.
2. Once the butter is melted, add the flour. Cook and stir for 5 to 6 minutes, or until the mixture is brown.
3. Add the caraway seeds, pepper and salt. Add the water gradually, stirring continuously. Continue to cook and stir for 20 to 30 minutes, or until the mixture is thick and smooth.
4. Drop the beaten eggs into the soup. Simmer for another 10 minutes.
5. Serve immediately and sprinkle with chervil or parsley.

Pumpkin Soup Bučova Juha

In Slovenia and its surrounding region, pumpkins are not generally used in cooking, as they are in the United States. In fact, it is very difficult to find fresh pumpkins in the markets in the fall. Neither is canned pumpkin available in the stores. In Slovenia, to find a pumpkin for a jack-o-lantern, pies, or even soups, one must visit a farm. There pumpkins are found in the pile of vegetables to be fed to the pigs. The farmer and his wife will happily give you as many pumpkins as you like, and shake their heads laughing as you walk away. Yet, pumpkin soup can still be found on menus in the fall. Sometimes it is peeled and boiled with broth, rather than pureed. This recipe for creamy pumpkin soup has some unique flavorings.

Serves 8

4 to 5 cups chicken stock
2 pounds pumpkin, peeled, seeded, and cubed
3 cloves garlic, peeled
2 medium onions, peeled and chopped
2 fresh tomatoes, chopped
2 bay leaves
¼ teaspoon dried marjoram
¼ teaspoon celery seeds
½ teaspoon dried thyme
1 teaspoon ground cinnamon
1 teaspoon salt, or to taste
Freshly ground pepper
1 cup heavy cream
Chopped parsley, for garnish

1. Place the chicken stock in a large saucepan over medium heat. Add all the other ingredients except the cream.

2. Cook over medium heat, covered, for 30 to 40 minutes, or until the pumpkin is soft. Remove from the heat. Remove the bay leaves.

3. If you prefer a creamier, smoother soup, mash the pumpkin mixture, or process it in batches in a food processor. Otherwise, leave the pumpkin as is.

4. Return the pumpkin mixture to the saucepan over medium heat. Slowly add the cream, stirring continuously. Continue cooking and stirring for 4 to 6 minutes, or until the soup is heated through. Do not let it boil.

5. Season to taste with salt and pepper. Garnish with parsley. Serve immediately.

Potato Soup Krompirjeva Juha

This soup is a tradition in the Prekmurje region of Slovenia, in the eastern part of the country near the border with Hungary. This is a creamy soup. The Hungarian version includes sour cream, always a nice touch.

Serves 4

3 pounds potatoes, washed, peeled, and cut into cubes
1 carrot, peeled and sliced
1 onion, peeled and chopped
1 quart milk or cream
4 tablespoons (½ stick) butter
1 teaspoon salt
Freshly ground pepper
1 teaspoon dried marjoram
Fresh parsley, chopped, for garnish

1. Fill a large saucepan with water. Add the salt.

2. Add the potatoes, carrot and onion to the water. Bring to a boil over high heat. Cook for 20 to 25 minutes, or until all the vegetables are soft.

3. Drain the water from the vegetables.

4. For a creamier, smoother soup, mash or puree the vegetables. If you prefer the vegetables in chunks, then leave them as is. Return the vegetables to the saucepan.

5. Add the milk or cream and butter to the vegetable mixture. Heat through over low to medium heat, stirring continuously.

6. Season to taste with salt, pepper and marjoram. Cook and stir for another few minutes. Serve hot with fresh parsley sprinkled on top of the soup.

Arno's Cream of Mushroom Soup

Gobova Kremna Juha

This soup is the signature dish of Gostilna pri Planincu, a guesthouse, pub and restaurant, run by Arno Pucher and his family since 1903, at the beginning of footpaths leading up to nearby Mount Triglav. People climbing the mountain frequently would stop for a glass of homemade blueberry schnapps and a hot bowl of the cream of mushroom soup.

Serves 8

2 tablespoons butter
2 onions, peeled and
  chopped
3 to 4 cloves garlic, minced
1½ pounds mushrooms
  (button, or a combination
  of portobello, shiitake,
  or oyster), sliced
1½ teaspoons salt
4 cups beef or vegetable
  broth
2 cups assorted vegetables
  (broccoli, carrots,
  cauliflower, potatoes), cut
  into small pieces
¼ teaspoon dried thyme
¼ teaspoon dried sage
¼ teaspoon dried tarragon
¼ teaspoon powdered
  mustard
1 cup sour cream
2 to 3 tablespoons
  all-purpose flour
1½ cups cream
Salt
Freshly ground black
  pepper
¼ cup chopped parsley
1 cup whipping cream,
  whipped, no sugar added

1. Melt the butter in a large saucepan. Add onions and garlic and cook, stirring continuously, over medium heat for 5 minutes. Stir in the mushrooms and salt. Continue to cook and stir over medium heat.

2. Once the mushrooms are tender, after about 10 minutes, add the beef stock, vegetables and herbs. Cook over medium heat for 20 to 30 minutes, or until the vegetables are tender.

3. In the meantime, in a small bowl, combine the sour cream and flour.

4. Slowly add the sour cream mixture to the hot soup, stirring continuously. Add the cream, stirring continuously.

5. Add salt and freshly ground pepper, to taste.

6. Remove the soup from the heat. Serve in bowls and top each with a spoonful of unsweetened whipped cream and a sprinkle of parsley.

7. Serve immediately with fresh bread and butter.

Garlic Soup Česena Juha

This recipe is also popular as a remedy for colds and flus in the winter months. (It may also keep away vampires.)

Serves 4

4 cups chicken broth (vegetable broth may also be used)
6 to 8 cloves garlic, peeled and crushed
1 bay leaf
¼ teaspoon dried sage
¼ teaspoon dried thyme
½ teaspoon salt
Freshly ground pepper
2 eggs, slightly beaten
¼ cup olive oil
⅓ cup Parmesan cheese, grated
4 slices French bread, slightly toasted
Chopped parsley, for garnish

1. In a large saucepan, bring the broth, garlic, and herbs to a boil. Cover, and simmer for 20 to 30 minutes.

2. Remove the soup from the heat. With a spoon, remove the bay leaf. If you wish, you may also strain the soup to remove the other herbs. Season to taste with salt and freshly ground pepper.

3. In a bowl, mix the eggs with the olive oil and Parmesan cheese.

4. Return the soup to low heat. Add the egg mixture to the soup in a slow drizzle, stirring continuously. Continue to stir the soup over low heat until it thickens. Do not overheat the soup, as the eggs may curdle.

5. Pour into soup bowls to serve. Place a piece of toast atop soup, and garnish with parsley.

Chestnut Soup Kostanjeva Juha

Throughout Eastern Europe, chestnuts are served in desserts and soups, and roasted on the street corners in the cool months of fall and early winter. Although they are difficult to prepare, their nutty, wintery taste provides a hearty base for this soup, which in Slovenia is traditionally considered a hangover cure for having drunk too much "young wine." Even today, Slovenians believe chestnut soup will "clear wine from the head."

Serves 6

½ pound chestnuts
4 cups chicken or
  vegetable broth
½ cup white wine
½ teaspoon salt
Freshly ground black
  pepper
½ teaspoon dried
  marjoram
½ teaspoon dried basil
¼ cup cider vinegar

1. To peel the chestnuts (a time-consuming job, for which there is no shortcut), cut a slit in each chestnut on the flat side of the nut. Drop several chestnuts at a time into a pan of boiling water. The heat will loosen the skins. Remove the chestnuts from the boiling water, let cool slightly, and remove the shells and skins with a small knife. Cut away any dark skin or moldy spots. If the skins are difficult to remove, you may drop them into the boiling water for a second time.

2. In a large saucepan, heat the broth with the peeled chestnuts over high heat, until boiling. Simmer over medium heat for 30 to 40 minutes, or until the chestnuts are softened.

3. Remove the chestnuts, and puree them in a food processor.

4. Return the chestnuts to the chicken broth. Add the remaining ingredients. Simmer for 15 minutes, or until heated through.

Koroška Wedding Soup Koroška Kremna Juha

This is a traditional dish from the Koroška region of Slovenia, located in the north, on the border of Austria. Today Koroška is Slovenia's smallest province, but it was once the center of the much larger Duchy of Greater Carinthia, which was established as the first Slavic state in the eighth century. Despite its historic democratic significance, the cuisine from the region is humble, reflecting the necessity to make do with what grows in this mountainous, valley terrain. This soup is a classic example of how the people of Koroška strive to make grand dishes for a special occasion (in this case, a wedding) from a mediocre piece of meat. Pig's feet, or hocks, can be obtained from your local butcher. Look for light pink to white meat, pink bones, and white fat, to identify fresh pieces. Spareribs, although certainly not traditional, are a good substitute.

Serves 8

4 cups water
2 teaspoons salt
2 pounds pig's feet
1 pound assorted soup
  vegetables (carrots,
  onions, parsnips, celery,
  turnips), peeled, if
  necessary, and cut into
  small pieces
3 or 4 cloves garlic, peeled
1 bay leaf
3 or 4 peppercorns
2 cups sour cream
½ cup all-purpose flour
1 or 2 egg yolks, slightly
  beaten

1. In a large saucepan, heat water and salt until it comes to a boil. Add the pig's feet, vegetables, garlic, bay leaf and peppercorns. Cook over medium to high heat for 30 to 40 minutes, or until the pig's feet are tender, and the meat is easy to take off the bone.

2. Remove the pig's feet from the stock. Remove the meat from the bones, and chop into small pieces.

3. In a bowl, mix the sour cream and flour.

4. Strain the stock to remove the vegetables and spices. Return the stock to the saucepan. Over medium heat, slowly add the sour cream mixture, stirring continuously.

5. Once the sour cream mixture is completely blended with the stock, slowly add the eggs, stirring continuously, until the soup is thickened. Return the meat to the soup and stir.

6. Serve immediately.

Chicken Soup with Liver Dumplings Kokošja Juha in Jetrni Cmoki

Liver Dumplings Jetrni Cmoki

½ pound chicken livers, rinsed, patted dry, and trimmed
1 egg
½ teaspoon salt
½ teaspoon oil
1 teaspoon finely chopped parsley
½ cup fine bread crumbs

1. Chop the livers finely, or process in a food processor.
2. Add the egg, salt, oil and parsley to the liver. Stir well.
3. Slowly add the bread crumbs to the liver mixture, stirring continuously, until a thick mixture is formed.
4. Set aside until the chicken soup is ready.

Chicken Soup Kokošja Juha

1 roasting chicken
  (3 to 4 pounds)
1 to 2 tablespoons salt
1 pound assorted soup vegetables (carrots, turnips, celery, cabbage, onions), peeled and cut into small pieces
1 bay leaf
4 or 5 peppercorns
2 garlic cloves, peeled
3 cloves

1. Place the chicken and all remaining ingredients for the soup in a large soup pot. Fill the pot with 4 to 5 cups water, or enough to completely cover the ingredients. Place over high heat and bring to a boil. Continue to simmer over medium heat, covered, for 2 hours, or until the chicken is tender.
2. Remove the soup from heat. Strain the broth into another pot. Put the chicken and vegetables to the side.
3. Bring the chicken broth to a boil.
4. Drop the liver mixture into the broth by the rounded teaspoonful. Continue to simmer, covered, for 10 minutes, until the dumplings are formed and cooked through.
5. Serve the soup hot. You may serve the meat and the vegetables on the side, or you may reserve them for another use.

Barley Soup Ričet

This is a traditional barley soup made with pork. Several parts of the pig may be used to flavor the soup: pig's feet, or ham hocks, as well as the pork neck or smoked ham. The soup is usually served with the sliced meat on the side.

Serves 8

1 cup dried pinto or pink beans, picked over and soaked in cold water overnight
2 pounds pork meat
1 cup barley
1 medium onion, peeled and quartered
2 cloves garlic, peeled and minced
2 or 3 carrots, peeled and cut into thick slices
1 bay leaf
3 or 4 peppercorns
Salt and freshly ground pepper

1. Over medium heat, cook the beans in the same water in which they soaked overnight for 30 to 35 minutes, or until the beans are cooked through. Remove from the heat and drain.

2. Place the meat in a large soup pot. Fill the pot with 2 quarts of water, or until the meat is covered. Cook over medium heat for 20 to 25 minutes, until the meat is cooked through. Remove the meat from the pot.

3. Add the barley, onion, garlic, carrots, bay leaf, and peppercorns to the pork broth. Cook over medium heat until the barley is cooked through, about another 20 to 30 minutes.

4. Add the beans, stir, and cook for a few more minutes over medium heat. Season to taste with salt and freshly ground pepper.

5. Serve the soup with slices of the meat on the side.

Carinthian Crayfish Soup

Jastog v Karantinski Juhi

This dish originates from the mountainous region of Gorenjska in northern Slovenia, where crayfish are found in the rivers. It is also served at the seaside on the Adriatic Coast; I enjoyed a wonderful version of this soup at the seaside restaurant Tri Vdove (The Three Widows) in Piran. If fresh crayfish are not available to you, shrimp or lobster may be used as a "seawater" substitute.

Serves 8

2 carrots, peeled and cut into large pieces
1 parsnip, peeled
3 or 4 stalks celery, cut into chunks
1 onion, peeled and quartered
1 bay leaf
2 teaspoons caraway seeds, or to taste
20 crayfish, scrubbed
1 or 2 cloves garlic, peeled and crushed
¼ pound (1 stick) butter
3 tablespoons all-purpose flour
¼ cup parsley, chopped, for garnish

1. In a large saucepan, cook the carrots, parsnip, celery, onion, bay leaf and caraway seeds in 4 to 5 cups of salted water for approximately 30 minutes.
2. Add the crayfish to the pot, and cook over high heat for 15 minutes.
3. Remove the crayfish from the pot. Let cool and remove the meat from the claws and tails. Crush the shells.
4. In a skillet, melt the butter. Add the garlic and cook for 2 to 3 minutes. Add the crushed crayfish shells, and fry until the butter turns red, about 4 to 5 minutes. Add the flour, and cook over medium heat, stirring continuously, until thickened. Add to the broth. Cook over medium heat, stirring continuously for 5 to 10 minutes, or until heated through.
5. Strain the soup and return it to the saucepan. (You may discard the vegetables and shells.) Bring to a boil. Add the crayfish meat that was removed from the shells, and the crayfish tails. Stir and heat through.
6. Serve immediately, sprinkled with parsley.

The logo for the Tri Vdove restaurant in Piran features
'The Three Widows.'

Pork and Pickled Turnip Stew Bujta Repa

The origin of the name of this recipe comes from the Slovenian word ubiti, *meaning "to slaughter." In the fall, pigs are slaughtered on the farm. During that season, people who live in the city traditionally buy a slaughtered pig from a farmer. Every bit of the pig is used: the feet, the blood (in sausages), as well as the meat. This sour stew was traditionally a way to use the abundance of fresh pork meat at slaughtering time.* Repa *means turnip. The recipe calls for sour turnips, which are made in brine, like sauerkraut. You may also use fresh turnips, cutting the vegetable into thick slices.*

Serves 8

½ pound pickled turnips
  or ½ pound fresh turnips,
  cut into thick slices
1½ pounds fresh pork
  meat (smoked pork meat
  may also be used)
½ cup millet, washed and
  picked over
2 tablespoons butter
2 tablespoons all-purpose
  flour
5 cloves garlic, peeled and
  chopped
1 small onion, peeled and
  chopped
½ cup sour cream
1 to 2 teaspoons salt
Freshly ground pepper
½ cup white wine vinegar,
  if using fresh turnips
½ teaspoon red paprika

1. Place the turnips and pork in a large pot. Fill with water just until the meat and turnips are covered. Cook over high heat for 35 to 45 minutes, or until the turnips are softened. Add the millet and stir. Bring to a boil.
2. In the meantime, melt the butter in a saucepan over medium heat. Stir in the flour to create a smooth paste. Add the garlic and onion to the butter-flour mixture and stir. Gradually add a little of the hot broth, and stir, forming a smooth mixture.
3. Add this mixture to the pork. Bring the stew to a boil. Slowly stir in the sour cream to thicken the stew.
4. Add salt and pepper to taste.
5. Lower the heat to medium and continue to cook for 30 to 35 minutes, or until the pork is cooked thoroughly.
6. Remove the pork from the stew and slice it.
7. If the turnips are not cooked through yet, continue to cook them without the pork, until they are tender.
8. If using fresh turnips, add the vinegar to the stew.

9. To serve, fill each plate or shallow soup bowl with the stew. Arrange the slices of pork on top. Sprinkle decoratively with paprika, if you wish.

Veal Stew Žvarcet

This is another rich, thick stew that goes well with red wine and will warm you up on a cool winter evening. There seems to be a combination of Hungarian and Italian influences in this dish, typical of the region, which makes for a tasty, hearty stew!

Serves 8

¼ pound (1 stick) butter
3 pounds veal meat, cut into cubes
1 cup fresh bread crumbs
4 cups beef broth
1 teaspoon grated nutmeg
1 teaspoon dried thyme
1 teaspoon dried marjoram
1 tablespoon chopped lemon rind
2 ounces Parmesan cheese, grated

1. In a large soup pot, melt half the butter over medium heat. Add the veal. Continue to cook over medium heat for about 15 minutes, or until the meat is browned.
2. In the meantime, melt the remaining butter in a small saucepan. Add the bread crumbs. Cook, stirring, until the bread crumbs are slightly browned, about 5 minutes.
3. Add the breadcrumb mixture to the meat. Add the beef broth, spices and lemon rind. Cook over low heat for 30 minutes, stirring occasionally. The stew should be thick.
4. Serve hot, sprinkled with the Parmesan cheese, with pasta, rice, or polenta.

Potato Soup with Kidney Beans and Sauerkraut Jota

This very traditional dish originates from the mild Primorska region of Slovenia, the western slice of the country that borders Italy and the Adriatic Coast. This thick soup, made with potatoes, kidney beans, and sauerkraut, has many variations. It is such a staple in the region that it is said in Primorska, a good cook is distinguished from a bad one by the quality of her jota.

Serves 8

1 pound potatoes, peeled and cut into small pieces
1 pound dried kidney beans, soaked in water overnight
1 medium onion, peeled and chopped
¼ pound bacon or smoked ham, cut into small pieces
½ cup all-purpose flour
½ pound sauerkraut or pickled turnips
1 bay leaf
2 cloves garlic, peeled and minced
1 medium tomato, chopped
½ to 1 teaspoon salt
Parsley or chives, chopped, for garnish
½ cup sour cream (optional)

1. In a medium saucepan, cook the potatoes for 20 to 25 minutes in boiling water to cover, or until they are soft. Drain the potatoes and save the water in which they were cooked.

2. Drain and rinse the soaked beans. In another saucepan, cook the beans in boiling water to cover for 20 to 30 minutes, or until soft. Drain the beans and save this water also.

3. In a large soup pot, cook and stir the onions and bacon over medium to high heat for 15 to 20 minutes, or until the onions are yellow and softened. Stir in the flour and continue cooking for another 5 to 6 minutes. Add ½ to 1 cup water, stirring continuously over medium heat, until the mixture is smooth.

4. Add the beans, potatoes and sauerkraut, plus the water that the beans and potatoes were cooked in. Add the bay leaf, garlic, tomato and salt.

5. Bring to a boil over medium to high heat. Continue to cook, stirring continuously, for 30 to 40 minutes, or until the soup reaches a slightly thick consistency.

6. Serve hot. Garnish with chopped parsley or chives and sour cream, if you wish.

Hungarian-Style Stew with Meat and Potatoes Bograč

Bograč is a traditional stew originating from the Prekmurje region of Slovenia, the far northeastern corner of the country. Prekmurje literally translates to "beyond the Mura," referring to the Mura River which divides this "forgotten" corner of the country from the rest of Slovenia. The region has a very strong Hungarian influence, due to its location at the border of Hungary. In Prekmurje, this rich meat and potato stew is made in a special clay pot served hanging over a flame, to keep the stew warm while it is eaten.

Serves 8

⅓ pound bacon,
  cut into small pieces
1 pound onions, peeled
  and chopped
2 red bell peppers, seeded
  and cut into small pieces
1 teaspoon ground sweet
  paprika
1 pound beef, cubed
  (stew meat is fine)
1 pound pork, cubed
2 pounds potatoes,
  peeled and quartered
2 cloves garlic,
  peeled and minced
¼ teaspoon caraway seeds
1 bay leaf
1 tablespoon tomato paste
½ to 1 teaspoon salt,
  or to taste

1. In a large soup pot, cook the bacon and onions over medium to high heat, stirring continuously.

2. When the onions are softened, after about 6 to 8 minutes, add the red peppers and the paprika. Continue to cook over medium heat, for another 4 to 5 minutes, or until the vegetables are cooked through, stirring often.

3. Add the beef and pork. Add enough water to just cover the meat. Simmer, covered, for about 1 hour.

4. Add the potatoes, garlic, caraway seeds, bay leaf, tomato paste and salt. Continue to cook, covered, for 30 minutes, or until the potatoes are cooked through.

5. Season the stew with salt to taste. Serve hot.

Vegetable Hot Pot Šara

Slovenian cuisine does not typically offer a lot of choices to vegetarians. However, this stew, made with butter, water, and vegetables, truly is a vegetarian dish. The traditional version calls for kohlrabi (in the cabbage family), turnips and potatoes but any combination of vegetables can be added, such as carrots, cauliflower, or broccoli.

3 pounds potatoes, peeled and cut into small pieces
2 medium kohlrabi, washed, peeled and cut into small pieces
4 medium turnips, peeled and cut into small pieces
¼ pound (1 stick) butter
½ cup all-purpose flour
½ to 1 teaspoon salt, or to taste
1 teaspoon paprika

1. In a large soup pot, cook the potatoes and kohlrabi in boiling salted water to cover until they are cooked through, about 20 minutes.
2. In a separate pot, cook the turnips in boiling salted water, until they are cooked through, about 20 minutes.
3. Drain the turnips and add them to the pot with the potatoes and kohlrabi, and the water in which the potatoes were cooked.
4. Melt the butter in a small skillet. Stir in the flour to create a smooth paste.
5. Slowly add the butter and flour mixture to the stew, stirring continuously. Salt to taste.
6. Serve hot and sprinkle with the paprika.

Fish Stew Brodet

This recipe comes from the coastal region of Slovenia. It is the Slovenian version of French bouillabaisse or Italian cioppino. You may use a variety of fish and shellfish for this recipe, mixing in several types of seafood gives the dish depth and flavor. In Slovenia, it is popular to have eel or squid as one of the ingredients. The stew goes well with white wine, such as a Riesling or Sauvignon Blanc.

Serves 8

2 pounds assorted white
   fish such as cod, scrod,
   or flounder, filleted and
   cut into 3-inch pieces
2 pounds assorted shellfish
   such as clams, mussels,
   shrimp
½ cup all-purpose flour
½ cup olive oil
1 medium onion,
   peeled and chopped
1 bunch parsley, washed,
   dried, and chopped
5 cloves garlic,
   peeled and minced
¼ cup tomato paste
½ cup white wine
Several slices lemon
Salt and freshly ground
   pepper

1. Coat the pieces of fish in flour.
2. Heat 3 tablespoons of the olive oil in a saucepan. Fry the fish in the oil for 4 to 5 minutes on each side, or until it is slightly browned all over. Remove the fried fish from the pan and place on a paper towel to drain.
3. In a large saucepan, heat the remaining olive oil. Add the onion and cook over medium heat for 3 to 4 minutes, or until softened and golden. Add the chopped parsley, garlic, and tomato paste to the onion. Continue to cook over medium heat, stirring often.
4. Add the shellfish to the onion mixture. Stir in ½ to 1 cup of water and bring to a boil. Reduce the heat and continue to simmer over medium heat for 20 minutes, or until the shellfish is cooked.
5. Add the fried fish, white wine, and lemon slices. Season with salt and freshly ground pepper.
6. Bring the stew to a boil and serve hot.

PLAYING GOLF IN SLOVENIA

Slovenia is the only country in the former Yugoslavia where golf has a history and is popular with the locals. The game is a favorite Slovenian sport, and helps to attract tourists from Italy, Germany, England, and even Asia. European professional events are held regularly at Bled Golf and Country Club. There are three eighteen-hole and several nine-hole golf courses throughout the country.

The golf course at Mokrice Castle, Golf Club Grad Mokrice, is truly a challenging and memorable course. Running through the former hunting grounds of the castle, the course is hilly, and presents such unusual challenges as pear orchards, the castle walls, and a local fishing hole. The first hole is a 370-yard par four that runs downhill from the outskirts of the castle grounds, past the caretaker's cottage. The following holes continue through the nearby valley, providing views of the Croatian border. The most challenging hole on the course is number 5. It is a short par four (three hundred and five yards) but a sharp dogleg left, turning at no less than a ninety-degree angle. To the right is a sharp-drop off with heavy shrubbery, and to the left, trees. A very straight tee shot is needed here, perfectly placed in the middle of a small landing area. The front nine ends with a hilly par five running alongside local farmland.

The back nine of Golf Club Mokrice begins with the famous par three tenth hole.

With an elevated tee, the 150-yard hole provides the castle wall as a backdrop. More often than not, spectators standing on the bridge over the castle moat will witness an errant tee shot hitting the castle wall, reversing direction, and landing gently on the green. The rest of the back nine runs past a local fishing pond, orchards, and riding stables. Narrow fairways lined with trees provide challenges to the fifteenth and sixteenth holes, and the eighteenth hole is a challenging finish with a 414-yard par four.

The original eighteen-hole golf course at Bled Golf and Country Club, the King's Course, was built between 1936 and 1938. One of the most beautiful courses in Europe, its location was chosen by the Austrian Rudolf von Gelmini. The views of the nearby snowcapped mountains are spectacular, and there are even views of Bled Castle from the back nine. The picturesque clubhouse, built in the style of a traditional Slovenian chalet, was built in 1940. In 1971, Donald Harradine was hired to help rebuild the eighteen-hole course. And in 1993, a new nine-hole course was built, the Lake Course, providing players with twenty-seven holes.

The King's Course is a well-designed and challenging course. Playing to six thousand, eight hundred and twenty yards from the championship tees, Bled is the site of European PGA events, the Slovenian Open, and other local tournaments. Gently rolling hills provide challenging shots as well as tremendous views of the nearby mountains. Elevated tees and wooded doglegs are the norm. The greens are well-maintained and roll well; they are also well-bunkered, providing challenging approach shots.

The Lake Course is much hillier than the King's Course, and, true to its name, there are several water hazards. In fact, the second and the ninth holes share the same green, which means hitting over the same lake. This course provides quite a workout for those who walk, and several blind shots for those looking for a challenge.

Finish your day of golf with lunch or a beer on the terrace of the Bled Clubhouse. Managed by the same group who run the Grand Hotel Toplice, its waiters are stylishly dressed in vests and bow ties. They serve local Union beer or cappuccino on silver trays. There is a delicious menu of local fare, along with a selection of Slovenian wines.

The cover of the scorecard from the Golf Club Grad Mokrice.

And whilst on the subject of salads, in those areas of Štajerska where hops are grown, especially in the Savinja Valley, a salad is prepared of cooked hop sprouts. Those who have tried it admit that they have tasted worse.

– From *Slovenian Cookery, Over 100 Classic Dishes,*
Edited by Tatjana Žener

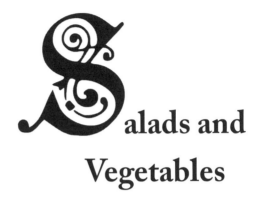

Salads and Vegetables

Po sadovih ocenjuj drevo, ne po listju.
Value a tree for its fruit, not its leaves.

– Slovenian proverb

Serbian Salad *Šopska Solata*

This salad is typical of the Balkan countries, where fresh tomatoes, peppers, and feta cheese are plentiful and richly flavorful.

Serves 6 to 8

Salad:
2 green bell peppers, seeded and chopped
2 red bell peppers, seeded and chopped
2 medium tomatoes, chopped
2 cucumbers, peeled and chopped
1 small onion, finely chopped
¼ cup chopped parsley (optional)
8 ounces feta cheese, crumbled (about 1½ cups), or fresh farmer cheese

Dressing:
¼ to ⅓ cup olive oil
2 to 3 tablespoons freshly squeezed lemon juice
1 teaspoon dried basil
½ teaspoon dried marjoram
¼ teaspoon dried oregano
Salt and freshly ground black pepper

1. Combine the peppers, tomatoes, cucumbers and onion in a salad bowl.
2. In a separate bowl, whisk together the olive oil, lemon juice, basil, marjoram, oregano, salt and pepper.
3. Pour the dressing over the vegetables. Mix well, and let chill.
4. Serve topped with the crumbled cheese. (Be generous!)

Hop Salad Hmeljova Solata

In Slovenia, hops are grown by local farmers, and are a key ingredient in each region's locally brewed beer. Hops have also found their way into the cuisine of the countryside. A seasonal item, they are eaten in the summer months when they are harvested. This is a simple recipe, one for the spring when the hops are just sprouting.

Serves 4

1 pound fresh hop sprouts
¼ cup vegetable oil
½ cup red wine vinegar
½ teaspoon salt, or to taste

1. In a saucepan, boil the hop sprouts in salted water for 10 to 15 minutes.
2. When the hop sprouts are softened, remove from the heat and drain. Let them cool.
3. Toss the sprouts with the oil, vinegar and salt, and serve immediately.

Dandelion Salad Regratova Solata

Young dandelion greens, picked early in the season, are tender and make a tasty salad. Once the flower buds are fully formed, the leaves become quite bitter. If you are picking the dandelion leaves yourself, look for the plants with the serrated leaves and the white shoots; they are the best for eating. The vinegar in the dressing is strong, to match the tartness of the greens. The warm dressing wilts the greens just enough to bring out their natural sweetness.

Serves 6

1 pound young dandelion
  greens, washed well and
  dried
2 medium potatoes,
  boiled, and sliced thinly
2 eggs, hard-boiled,
  peeled and sliced
3 or 4 strips bacon
2 or 3 tablespoons red
  wine vinegar or balsamic
  vinegar
1 tablespoon olive oil
½ teaspoon salt, or to taste
Freshly ground pepper

1. Pick through the dandelion greens, removing stems and selecting the most tender leaves. Place them in a salad bowl.
2. Add the sliced potatoes and eggs to the salad.
3. In a skillet, cook the bacon until it is crisp. Drain on paper towels reserving drippings. Cut or crumble the bacon into small pieces. Add to the salad.
4. Sprinkle several spoonfuls of the warm bacon fat on the salad. Add the vinegar, olive oil, salt and pepper. Toss and serve immediately.

Mixed Salad Mešana Solata

The flavorful Slovenian salads are a refreshing treat for travelers to the region. A popular item in Slovenian restaurants, a "mixed salad" is a variety of vegetable salads grouped on a bed of lettuce. A plate may arrive with greens and a small portion each of tomato salad, cucumber salad, marinated beets, beans, potato salad, peppers, or cabbage salad. With fresh bread, a *mešana solata* can make a meal! The following are some of the salads you may want to try when making your own Slovenian mixed salad. Try different combinations, and create your own variations.

Beet Salad Rdeča Pesa

This salad will have a little bite to it, from the fresh horseradish. Prepared horseradish is an acceptable substitute for the fresh version, but will provide a different kind of flavor. This salad goes well in a mixed salad, or can be served as a side dish with sausages, pork, or ham.

Serves 4

2 pounds medium beets
1 tablespoon caraway seeds
¼ cup cider vinegar
1 teaspoon salt
1 tablespoon sugar
2 tablespoons vegetable oil
1 tablespoon freshly grated horseradish

1. Cook the beets with the caraway seeds in salted water over low heat until they are tender, about 30 to 45 minutes.
2. Remove the beets from the heat, drain and let them cool.
3. Peel and slice the beets and place them in a salad bowl. Add the vinegar, salt, sugar, oil and horseradish. Mix well.
4. Cover and let marinate in the refrigerator for several hours before serving.
5. Add salt to taste and serve.

Green Salad _Zelena Solata_

Serves 4 to 6

**1 head Boston lettuce,
  torn into bite-size pieces**
**⅓ cup lemon juice or white
  vinegar**
¼ cup vegetable oil
⅓ cup cream or milk
½ teaspoon salt
1 teaspoon sugar
Freshly ground pepper
**Chives, cleaned and
  chopped, for garnish
  (optional)**

1. Place the lettuce in a salad bowl.
2. In a separate bowl or cup, combine the lemon juice, oil, cream, salt, sugar and pepper. Stir well.
3. Toss the greens with the dressing. Sprinkle with chives, if so desired. Serve immediately.

Cabbage Salad _Zeljnata Solata_

Serves 4 to 6

**1 small head cabbage,
  outer leaves discarded,
  shredded or sliced thinly**
⅓ cup cider vinegar
¼ cup vegetable oil
1 teaspoon salt
1 tablespoon sugar
**1 teaspoon caraway seeds,
  ground**

1. Place the cabbage in a salad bowl.
2. In a small bowl, whisk together the vinegar, oil, salt, sugar and caraway seeds. Mix well.
3. Just before serving, toss the cabbage with the dressing.

Cucumber Salad Kumarična Solata

Serves 4

Freshly ground pepper
1 teaspoon salt
2 teaspoons sugar
2 tablespoons cider vinegar
  or tarragon vinegar
1 tablespoon vegetable oil
2 medium cucumbers,
  peeled and sliced as
  thinly as possible
1 small onion (red or
  white), peeled and
  minced
½ cup sour cream
  (optional)
Chopped parsley or chives,
  for garnish

1. In a salad bowl, combine the pepper, salt, sugar, vinegar and oil. Mix well.
2. Add the cucumbers and onion. Mix well.
3. Cover and refrigerate for at least one hour before serving.
4. To serve, top with sour cream and/or parsley, as desired.

Green Bean Salad Stročji Fižolova Solata

Serves 4 to 6

1 pound green beans,
  trimmed
1 medium onion,
  peeled and minced
⅓ cup sugar
½ cup cider vinegar
⅓ cup vegetable oil
1 teaspoon salt
½ teaspoon freshly ground
  pepper, or to taste

1. Cook the green beans in salted water over high heat for 3 to 5 minutes, or until just tender. The beans should still be slightly crisp; they should not be soft or mushy. Remove from heat, drain, and let the beans cool.
2. In a salad bowl, whisk together the onion, sugar, vinegar, oil, salt and pepper.
3. Once the beans have cooled completely, add them to the salad bowl and toss with the dressing. Cover and let stand at room temperature for at least 1 hour before serving.

Slovenian Potato Salad Krompirjeva Solata

Serves 4 to 6

2 pounds potatoes
1 medium onion,
  peeled and chopped
½ cup cider vinegar
¼ cup vegetable oil
1 egg
1 to 2 teaspoons salt,
  or to taste
2 teaspoons sugar
Freshly ground pepper
Chopped fresh parsley
  for garnish

1. Boil the potatoes in salted water for 20 to 25 minutes, or until they are tender and cooked all the way through. Drain. When able to be handled, peel them and slice thinly.
2. In a large salad bowl, combine the onion, vinegar, oil, egg, salt, sugar and pepper.
3. Add the warm potato slices to the salad bowl. Toss well with the dressing. Add more vinegar or oil, as desired. The potatoes will soak up the dressing. Cover and let sit for 1 hour.
4. Before serving, sprinkle with chopped parsley. Serve slightly warm or cool.

Apple and Celery Salad Solata z Jabolki in Zeleno

Serves 4

Salad:
1 head endive, cleaned and separated
3 tart, red apples such as Macoun, McIntosh or Cortland, cored and sliced thin
1 stalk celery, cut into chunks
¼ pound smoked Gouda cheese, or any other hard cheese, sliced thin
¼ cup hazelnuts, toasted
Black olives, for garnish (optional)

Dressing:
3 tablespoons olive oil
2 tablespoons Dijon mustard
Juice of 1 lemon (about 2 tablespoons)
1 shallot or small onion, peeled and minced
½ teaspoon salt
Freshly ground pepper

1. Arrange the salads on individual plates: Begin by arranging 2 to 3 endive leaves on each plate. Then sprinkle the apples, celery, cheese and hazelnuts on top of the endive.
2. In a small bowl, whisk together the olive oil, mustard, lemon juice, shallot or onion, salt and pepper.
3. Just before serving, drizzle the dressing over the salads. Garnish with the black olives, if desired.

Asparagus Vinaigrette Beluši Vinaigret

This is another one of the many asparagus dishes served during the "Days of Asparagus" in early summer at the restaurant of Pension Mayer in Bled.

Serves 4 as an appetizer

1 bunch (about 1 pound) asparagus, tough ends removed
3 to 4 tablespoons olive oil
1 tablespoon Dijon mustard
2 tablespoons cider vinegar or red wine vinegar
½ teaspoon salt
Freshly ground pepper

1. Cook the asparagus in salted water until tender, but still crisp (about 4 to 5 minutes). Do not let the asparagus get too soft or mushy. Remove from heat, drain, and let the asparagus cool.

2. In a bowl, whisk together the olive oil, mustard, vinegar, salt and pepper.

3. When the asparagus has cooled, toss with the dressing. You may serve this as an appetizer, a salad, or a side dish.

Sautéed Turnip Leaves Praženi Repni Listi

Serves 4

1 bunch (about 1 pound)
  young turnip leaves,
  well washed and
  stemmed
5 tablespoons butter
3 or 4 cloves garlic,
  peeled and sliced thin
2 tablespoons chopped
  fresh parsley
½ teaspoon salt
Freshly ground pepper
2 to 3 tablespoons freshly
  grated Parmesan cheese,
  for garnish

1. Steam the turnip leaves over boiling water until they are slightly wilted. Chop them into bite-size pieces.

2. In a skillet, melt the butter. Cook the garlic and parsley, stirring occasionally, until the garlic is golden brown.

3. Add the turnip leaves and salt. Continue to cook over medium heat, stirring continuously, until the turnip leaves are tender, 5 to 8 minutes.

4. Remove the turnip leaves from the heat. Season with salt and pepper, to taste. Serve sprinkled with the Parmesan cheese.

Sweet and Sour Red Cabbage

Prislijeno Redeče Zelje

Also a popular dish in Austria and Germany, this side dish is a wonderful complement to meat and pork dishes.

Serves 4 as a side dish

2 tablespoons butter
1 large onion, peeled
   and chopped
2 tart apples, peeled,
   cored, and chopped
1 head red cabbage,
   quartered, cored and
   shredded
2 to 3 tablespoons sugar
¼ to ⅓ cup vinegar,
   or to taste
1 cup red wine or water
½ teaspoon salt
Pepper to taste
1 to 2 tablespoons
   all-purpose flour

1. In a large skillet, melt the butter. Add the onions, and cook, stirring occasionally, until soft.

2. Add the apples and cabbage to the onions. Cook over medium-high heat, stirring occasionally, until the cabbage and apples are coated in butter.

3. Add the sugar, vinegar, and wine. Stir until all the ingredients are combined. Make sure that most of the cabbage is covered with liquid.

4. Continue cooking until bubbling. Cover and let simmer over medium to low heat for 30 to 45 minutes, until the cabbage is tender.

5. Season with salt and pepper. Sprinkle with flour. Stir over medium heat until a thick liquid is formed, about 5 minutes.

6. Add additional sugar or vinegar to taste, and serve.

Sauerkraut

Kislo Zelje

Sauerkraut, marinated cabbage, is a staple of the Germanic cuisines. Fresh sauerkraut can be bought packaged in most supermarkets. However, the tastiest sauerkraut can be found in barrels at large delis or gourmet markets. On a Saturday morning in the vegetable market in Ljubljana, one can see long lines of people waiting at the stand with the "best" sauerkraut in the city. On the next pages are some ways you may want to try preparing sauerkraut. In Slovenia, it is served as a side dish to pork, other meats, or sausages. It can also be served on its own as a vegetarian dish.

Baked Sauerkraut Pečeni Kislo Zelje

This dish can be served as a side dish to meat, or on its own with potatoes for lunch. Remove the meat, and it can be served as a vegetarian dish.

Serves 6 to 8 as a side dish

2 pounds sauerkraut
  (preferably fresh)
2 tablespoons lard, melted
  butter or oil
3 or 4 slices bacon
¼ pound ham, sliced
1 teaspoon peppercorns
1 teaspoon juniper berries
1 teaspoon caraway seeds
1 cup white wine

1. In a large saucepan, cook the sauerkraut over medium heat until it comes to a boil.
2. Remove from the heat and drain. Return to the saucepan, and drizzle with 1 tablespoon of the melted fat.
3. Line the bottom of a rectangular baking dish with the slices of bacon.
4. On top of the bacon, form a layer of sauerkraut using about ¼ to ⅓ of the sauerkraut.
5. On top of the sauerkraut, form a layer of ham, peppercorns and juniper berries.
6. Continue layering the sauerkraut with the ham, peppercorns and juniper berries, until the ingredients are all used.
7. Sprinkle the top with the caraway seeds and drizzle the remaining 1 tablespoon of fat and the wine over the sauerkraut.
8. Bake at 350°F for about 30 minutes, or until the sauerkraut has turned slightly yellow.

Fried Sauerkraut Ocvrti Kislo Zelje

Serves 8 as a side dish

2 pounds sauerkraut
1 stalk celery, chopped
  (optional)
1 medium onion, peeled
  and chopped (optional)
1 carrot, peeled and sliced
  (optional)
8 tablespoons lard, butter,
  or oil
¼ cup all-purpose flour
3 or 4 cloves garlic, peeled
  and crushed
1 teaspoon salt
Freshly ground pepper

1. In a large saucepan, heat the sauerkraut over medium heat until boiling. Add a little water, if necessary. If you wish, you may add the other vegetables (celery, onion, carrot) now. Continue to cook for 10 to 15 minutes.
2. In a skillet, heat the fat until it is melted. Stir in the flour, and form a thick sauce.
3. Add the garlic and stir. Cook for 1 to 2 minutes.
4. Add the flour mixture to the sauerkraut and stir. Continue to cook over medium heat, stirring occasionally, until a thick sauce has formed, about 10 to 12 minutes.
5. Season with salt and freshly ground pepper. Serve with sausages or pork, if so desired.

Sauerkraut with Potatoes

Kislo Zelje s Krompirjem

Serves 8

½ pound potatoes, boiled,
  peeled, and mashed, with
  some cooking water
  reserved
2 pounds sauerkraut
2 tablespoons lard, butter,
  or oil
2 tablespoons all-purpose
  flour
1 medium onion,
  peeled and chopped
1 teaspoon salt
Freshly ground pepper

1. To the prepared potatoes, add a little of the water they were cooked in, to make them creamy. Set aside.

2. In a large saucepan, cook the sauerkraut over medium heat with a little water, until boiling.

3. In a skillet, heat the fat until it is melted. Stir in the flour, and form a thick sauce. Add the chopped onion, and stir, cooking for another 3 to 5 minutes.

4. Drain the sauerkraut, and return to the saucepan. Stir in the flour mixture, and continue to cook over medium heat, stirring occasionally, until a thick sauce is formed.

5. Add the mashed potatoes and stir. Continue to cook over medium heat for 10 to 15 minutes.

6. Season with salt and freshly ground pepper, as desired.

LJUBLJANA, THE BELOVED CITY

Ljubljana is the capital of Slovenia, as well as the center of its soul and spirit. Named for the word *ljubljena* meaning "beloved," this beautiful city truly is beloved by Slovenians, and by visitors from everywhere. It is a quaint city with cobblestone streets, outdoor markets, sidewalk cafés, and baroque churches; art nouveau bridges cross the Ljubljanica River, which winds through the center of town. Sometimes referred to as a "little Prague," Ljubljana also features a castle overlooking the old town, a wonderful display of art nouveau architecture, street musicians, and many fantastic restaurants. As the nation's capital, Ljubljana has always been at the crossroads between West and East. Now, with Slovenia's recent integration into the European Union, Ljubljana is a rising star for visitors to Central Europe.

The first reference to Ljubljana in writing was as "Laibach," in 1144. However, many had been there before that time including the Celts, who were established there in about 400 BC. The Romans established it as "Emona," which became a thriving town by 100 BC. Remains of Roman walls, churches, and other dwellings still exist around the city. Emona was destroyed by the Huns in the fifth century; and in the sixth century, Slavic tribes settled there. Ljubljana became the capital city for the Duchy of Carinthia in the twelfth century, and in 1335 was taken over by the Habsburgs who, with one exception, ruled

Ljubljana until the end of World War I in 1918. The only time the Habsburgs lost control of Ljubljana was when Napoleon made it the capital of the Illyrian provinces, from 1809 to 1813.

In the mid-1800s, Ljubljana became the center of Slovenian nationalism, while Slovenia remained under Austrian rule. National writers such as France Prešeren and Ivan Cankar produced most of their work there. In 1895, an earthquake struck the city, and much rebuilding occurred. Ljubljana benefited from this, as art nouveau-style architecture was all the rage in Central Europe at this time, and many beautiful buildings were constructed. Although many of them were destroyed under communist rule (their beauty and detail were considered "frivolous"), many do remain. Some have been neglected over the years, however many others, such as the Hotel Union, have been restored with great care and precision.

Art nouveau was an art style that developed all over Europe at the turn of the twentieth century, marking the beginning of modern art. Breaking away from traditional styles, art nouveau embraced all forms of art, including painting, sculpture, and architecture. Art nouveau developed lighter and more liberal forms of expression, and sought inspiration from nature, flowers and the animal kingdom, folklore, exotic cultures, geometrical forms, and national motifs. The main theme of art nouveau was that all art was treated equally, and that all people should have access to it, the middle class as well as nobility. The highest goal of art nouveau was to create total works of art, called *Gesamtkunstwerke*, whereby a variety of art works blend together to become a harmonious whole. In the late 1800s, art nouveau architects took advantage of new technology available at the time, such as steel-reinforced concrete, to build railway stations, banks, bridges, department stores, markets, schools, and other structures. The use of this architectural style for public buildings went along with the theme that art belonged to everyone. The secessionist school of art nouveau arrived in Ljubljana in the early 1890s. The first art nouveau structure was the Dragon Bridge (*Zmajski most*), which remains today as the symbol of Ljubljana. Other gems of art nouveau architecture in Ljubljana are the buildings that surround Prešeren Square, in the center of the city; the Centromerkur, the first department store in Ljubljana; the Mestna Hranilnica, the first savings bank in Slovenia established in 1882; and many schools, theaters, bridges, and residential buildings. One can do an "art nouveau" walking tour of Ljubljana and see ornate and beautiful building facades, tile mosaics, ironwork in railings, glasswork in windows, and stone sculpture on bridges.

After World War I, Slovenia joined the Kingdom of Serbs, Croats, and Slovenes. During World War II, Ljubljana was occupied by the Italians and then the Germans. The latter surrounded the city with a wall of barbed wire, essentially turning it into an "urban concentration camp." Today one can walk or jog around the city on a path that is on the site of this old wall. At the close of the war, Ljubljana became the capital of the Socialist Republic of Slovenia under Yugoslavia, established in 1945, and remained the capital when Slovenia declared independence in 1991. Today the city hosts a well-known

International Music Festival every year, and many concerts. It is also the site of Ljubljana University, beautiful parks, museums and galleries, shops, cafés, and wonderful restaurants. It is certainly well worth a visit!

The coat of arms of the Duchy of Carinthia.

THE DUCHY OF CARINTHIA

oday Koroška (Carinthia, in English) is a small region in northern Slovenia. However, years ago, it was the core of Greater Carantania, the Slovenian republic stretching as far north as Austria, and as far south as the Croatian port of Rijeka. Its center was at Krn Castle (Karburg) now called Klagenfurt, in southern Austria.

In the early eighth century, a new class of Slavs emerged in Carinthia who elected their own leaders. An ancient ritual surrounding the crowning of the new leader included the election of a free farmer by his peers, to question the new duke on his integrity. The *knez*, or grand duke, was publicly elected and crowned on the *knežji kame*, or duke's rock, in the courtyard of Krn Castle. It was a mainly symbolic delegation of power from the people to their leader: In the words of the people, "We give you the power, you give us the protection and rights, and together we shall work towards achieving common prosperity."

This early form of democracy was described in 1576 by French political philosopher Jean Bodin in his publication *Six livres de la Republic*. Bodin wrote in *The Genesis of Contractual Theory and the Installation of the Dukes of Carinthia* that the installation of Carinthian leaders had no equal in the world, and formed the roots of modern democracy. In fact, it is believed that Thomas Jefferson was influenced by the Carinthian coronation after reading about it in Bodin's work. He would incorporate elements of it in his *Contractual Theory* and in the writing of the U.S. Declaration of Independence.

The last such coronation in Carinthia was in 1414. Carinthia was then incorporated into the Frankish, and later the German, empire. However, its influence on Slovenian and other democracies remains today.

Potatoes, Rice, and Pasta

Male cooks–in contrast to their diligent, clean and fair female counterparts–believe that they are more clever and try to outwit the women-folk; and what has been the consequence of this? They have, indeed, invented all sorts of dishes, but dishes harmful to one's health. They have introduced a whole variety of un-healthy foods hidden behind a cloak of fancy names.

– Valentin Vodnik, Slovenian poet,
from the introduction to his cookbook,
1799

Potatoes with Pork Cracklings

Krompir z Ocvirki

Potatoes (krompirs) *are a staple in Slovenian cuisine. They are served boiled, fried, baked, in tortes, and with cheese. They often serve as a complement to meat dishes. The following are traditional potato recipes as well as a few modern ones.*

Serves 6 as a side dish

2 pounds potatoes, peeled or scrubbed, and halved
½ cup pork cracklings or 4 slices of bacon
Salt
Freshly ground pepper

1. Cook the potatoes in salted water over high heat until they are tender and cooked all the way through. Drain.
2. If you are using bacon, fry in a skillet over medium to high heat until crispy. Remove the bacon slices and drain on paper towels. Reserve the fat in the pan.
3. Just before serving, crumble the bacon over the potatoes, and drizzle the potatoes with the bacon fat. (If you are using pork cracklings, do the same with the pork.)
4. Season to taste with salt and pepper.

Fried Potatoes Pražen Krompir

You may use leftover boiled potatoes for this recipe.

Serves 6

2 pounds potatoes,
  scrubbed or peeled
5 tablespoons lard,
  butter or oil
2 medium onions,
  peeled and chopped
1 to 2 teaspoons salt
Freshly ground pepper
¼ to ½ cup beef broth

1. Cook the potatoes in salted water over medium to high heat for 15 to 20 minutes, or until they are tender. Drain and let cool.
2. Heat the fat in a skillet. Cook the onions over medium heat, stirring occasionally, until translucent.
3. Slice the potatoes. Add them to the pan and sprinkle with the salt and pepper. Cook over medium heat, stirring occasionally, for 15 to 20 minutes, until nicely browned on each side. Add some of the beef broth to the potatoes as they are cooking, a few tablespoons at a time.
4. Season to taste with salt and pepper. Serve hot.

Mashed Potatoes Krompirjev Pire

Serves 6 as a side dish

2 pounds potatoes, peeled
  or scrubbed, and halved
5 tablespoons butter
¾ cup whole milk or cream
1 to 2 teaspoons salt
Freshly ground pepper
Fresh parsley, washed,
  dried and chopped,
  for garnish

1. Cook the potatoes in salted water over high heat for 20 minutes, or until they are cooked all the way through and flake when you prick them with a fork. Drain and mash.
2. Add the butter, milk, salt and pepper. Stir until smooth. Add more milk or butter, if desired, to get a smoother, creamy consistency.
3. Season to taste with salt and pepper and sprinkle with the parsley. Serve warm.

Potatoes with Cottage Cheese Čompe

A simple recipe, this dish is often found in both the Primorska (by the sea) and Gorenjska (Alpine) regions of the country.

Serves 6 as a side dish

2 pounds potatoes, scrubbed
2 cups cottage cheese or fresh farmer cheese
4 or 5 tablespoons butter
1 teaspoon salt
Freshly ground pepper

1. Cook the potatoes in salted water over medium to high heat for 15 to 20 minutes, or until they are tender.
2. Let the cottage cheese drain in a strainer for ½ hour or so.
3. Drain the potatoes. Smother with butter while the potatoes are still warm. Season with salt and pepper, as you desire.
4. Serve with the cottage cheese.

Potatoes with Walnut Sauce

Krompir z Orehovo Omako

The sauce for these potatoes is like a coarse walnut pesto. It is delicious!

Serves 6 as a side dish

1½ cups walnuts, chopped
½ cup grated Parmesan
  cheese
2 small cloves garlic,
  peeled and minced
½ cup fresh basil or
  parsley, washed, dried
  and chopped
1 tablespoon olive oil
1 teaspoon salt
Freshly ground pepper
2 pounds potatoes,
  scrubbed and halved

1. In a small bowl, combine the walnuts, Parmesan, garlic, basil or parsley, olive oil, salt and pepper. Cover and let stand for half an hour.
2. Cook the potatoes in salted water over high heat for 15 to 20 minutes, or until they are tender. Drain. Place them in a bowl and toss with the walnut sauce. Season with more salt and pepper, if you desire. Serve warm or cold.

Polenta *Polenta*

Polenta (a type of cornmeal) is traditionally an Italian dish. It can be served many ways–boiled, grilled, or fried. It can also be served with a variety of sauces or meat dishes. The following is a basic recipe for polenta, using a cold-water method. Be careful to stir continuously, so that no lumps form. Try polenta with Golaž, page 128.

Serves 6 as a side dish

5 cups cold water
1 tablespoon salt
**1½ cups coarse polenta
(not to be confused with
regular cornmeal)**
**3 to 4 tablespoons butter,
or to taste**

1. Combine the water and salt in a large saucepan.
2. Stirring continuously, add the cornmeal in a slow, steady stream. Stir until the polenta is uniformly distributed.
3. Place the saucepan over medium heat and cook, stirring continuously. Always stir in the same direction, to avoid lumps.
4. Once the mixture is stiff and pulls away from the pan, stir in the butter.
5. Serve the polenta right away, as is, or place in a buttered baking dish. Once the polenta has hardened, you may slice it into pieces to serve with your favorite sauce, goulash or other meat dish. Or grill or fry the polenta slices.

Cooked Cornmeal Žganci

Žganci is a very traditional Slovenian dish. It can be served as a savory dish, with pork cracklings or lard, or as a sweet dish, with warm milk or honey.

Serves 6

3 cups flour (cornmeal, maize, strong wheat)
4 cups water
2 teaspoons salt
¼ cup lard or pork cracklings, heated
1 cup milk, warmed (optional)
½ cup honey (optional)

1. Bring the water and salt just to a boil in a medium saucepan. Add the flour as soon as the water begins to boil. Continue to cook at medium heat for 15 to 20 minutes.
2. When the flour has formed a large ball, prick the ball with a fork. Break the ball apart and turn it over, so that the inside of the žganci will also cook. Continue to cook for another 10 minutes.
3. Drain most of the water from the žganci, leaving some water, so that the žganci is not dry.
4. Drizzle the žganci with the fat.
5. If serving a savory žganci, serve as is. If serving a sweet dish, serve with honey or milk, as desired.

Potato Gnocchi with Wild Mushroom Cream Sauce

Njoki z Marcnicami in Smetano

Serves 6 as a side dish or starter

Gnocchi:
2 pounds starchy potatoes, scrubbed
1½ to 2 cups all-purpose flour
3 to 4 tablespoons butter, softened
1 teaspoon salt
¼ teaspoon freshly ground pepper

Sauce:
1 pound fresh mushrooms (wild or cultivated)
1 tablespoon butter
1 tablespoon all-purpose flour
½ teaspoon salt
Freshly ground pepper
¼ cup sour cream
2 egg yolks
Juice of ½ lemon
1 tablespoon fresh chopped parsley

1. Cook the potatoes in salted water over high heat for 15 to 20 minutes, or until they are tender.

2. Drain the potatoes and set aside to cool, slightly. While the potatoes are still warm, peel and mash.

3. While the potatoes are still warm, add 1½ cups of the flour and the butter, salt and pepper. Mix to form a soft dough. If the dough is sticky, add more flour—add as much flour as you need to in order to form a dough that you can work with.

4. On a floured surface, knead the dough for 10 to 15 minutes. Divide the dough into four parts. Shape each piece into a long roll, about 12 inches long. Cut the rolls into 1½ inch slices. Allow them to rest.

5. Roll each little gnocchi, or piece of dough, over the surface of a grater, to give them an interesting pattern.

6. Fill a saucepan three-quarters full with salted water. Cook the gnocchi in the water until they rise to the top of the pan, about 8 to 10 minutes. Drain.

7. To make the sauce, wash the mushrooms well and dry them. In a skillet, melt the butter, and cook the mushrooms over medium heat for 12 to 15 minutes or until there is no liquid left in the pan. Add the flour, salt and pepper. Continue to cook, stirring, over medium heat for another 5 to 6 minutes.

8. In a small bowl, whisk together the sour cream, egg yolks and lemon juice. Toss the mushrooms with the sour cream mixture.
9. Serve the gnocchi warm, covered with the mushroom sauce and sprinkled with the parsley.

Chestnut Gnocchi Kostanjevi Svaljki

The chestnuts give the gnocchi a rich, nutty flavor. Serve simply with melted butter and sprinkled with sugar.

Serves 4 as a side dish

1 pound chestnuts
4 eggs
½ cup all-purpose flour
8 tablespoons butter
  (1 stick), softened
¼ cup sugar
½ teaspoon salt

1. To cook and peel the chestnuts, drop into a pot of boiling water. Let cook for 10 to 15 minutes. When the chestnuts are tender, remove them from the water and drain. Let the chestnuts cool slightly. While they are still warm, remove the skins.
2. Chop the chestnuts, or process them in a food processor until they are in small pieces.
3. In a large bowl, combine the chestnuts with the eggs, flour, butter, sugar and salt, until it forms a workable dough. If the dough is too sticky, you may add more flour.
4. On a floured surface, knead the dough for 10 to 15 minutes.
5. Divide the dough into 3 or 4 parts. Form a long roll with each piece of dough. Cut the rolls into 1½ inch pieces. Allow them to rest for 15 to 20 minutes. (If you like, you may roll the gnocchi, or slices of dough, over the surface of a grater, to decorate them.)
6. Fill a saucepan three-quarters full with salted water. Cook the gnocchi in the water until they rise to the top of the pan. Drain.
7. Serve drizzled with melted butter, and sprinkled with sugar if desired.

Cheese Štruklji Sirovi Štruklji

Štruklji are traditional rolled dumplings that are very popular in this region of the former Yugoslavia. Each area of Slovenia and Croatia has its most popular version of štruklji. For example, some people like their štruklji boiled, some baked, some in soup. A variety of fillings can be added to the rolled dough. Štruklji can be served as a side dish with meat, as an appetizer, or as a main dish. Cheese-filled štruklji have been popular with Catholics as a main meal on Fridays, when they were not allowed to eat meat. Sweet versions of štruklji with apples and raisins are also served as dessert or with coffee in the afternoons. These sweet dumplings are also popular as dinner for children. What follows is a typical version of cheese štruklji.

Serves 6

Dough:
1 egg
2 tablespoons vegetable oil
1 teaspoon salt
1 tablespoon vinegar
½ to 1 cup warm water
3 cups all-purpose flour

Filling:
8 tablespoons butter
   (1 stick), softened, plus 4
   tablespoons, melted
4 eggs, slightly beaten
1 pound cottage cheese
1 cup sour cream
½ teaspoon salt

Topping:
½ cup fresh bread crumbs
4 tablespoons (½ stick)
   butter

1. To make the dough, combine in a large bowl all the ingredients for the dough, except the flour. Slowly add the flour, stirring continuously. Form a soft, workable dough. If the dough is too dry, add more warm water. If the dough is too sticky, add more flour.
2. Knead the dough on a floured surface for 10 to 15 minutes.
3. Divide the dough into 3 equal parts, and place the dough in a greased bowl. Coat each piece of dough with a thin film of vegetable oil. Cover and let stand in a warm, protected place for 1 to 2 hours.
4. To make the filling, mix together the softened butter, eggs, cottage cheese, sour cream and salt.
5. To prepare the štruklji, cover a table with a large, clean cloth or thin towel. Sprinkle it with flour. Roll out one of the pieces of dough on the cloth as thinly as you can. Continue to pull the dough with your hands until it is paper-thin. Trim away the thick edges of the dough. Brush it with the melted butter.

6. Spread one-third of the filling on one-half of the dough. Roll up like a jelly roll. Take a wooden spoon, and cut the roll into 4-inch pieces, sealing the edges with the wooden spoon. Make sure all the edges of the štruklji are sealed.

7. Continue to make štruklji with the remaining dough and filling.

8. To cook the štruklji, place 2 or 3 at a time in a pot of boiling salted water, and cook for 15 to 20 minutes. Remove the štruklji from the pot with a slotted spoon. Place on a serving plate.

9. To prepare the topping, melt the 4 tablespoons of butter in a skillet over medium heat. Add the bread crumbs and continue to cook over medium heat, stirring occasionally, until the bread crumbs are browned.

10. Serve the štruklji smothered with the bread crumbs, and more melted butter, if you wish.

Plum Dumplings Češpljevi Cmoki

Cmoki are another type of dumpling often served in Slovenia. They can be savory, such as bread dumplings, or sweeter, such as those filled with fruit. They are often served as a side dish with meat, or on their own with melted butter. The following recipe for plum dumplings includes a plum sauce for the topping. Plum dumplings are sometimes served on their own in ski lodges as a warm, filling lunch.

Makes approximately 20 dumplings

Dough:
5 large potatoes, peeled
4 tablespoons (½ stick) butter, softened
1 egg, slightly beaten
½ teaspoon salt
1 to 1½ cups all-purpose flour

Filling:
20 to 25 fresh Italian plums, pitted, unpeeled
2 to 3 tablespoons sugar
1 to 2 tablespoons ground cinnamon

Sauce:
20 fresh Italian plums, pitted, unpeeled
½ cup plus 1 tablespoon sugar
2 teaspoons ground cinnamon
¼ cup water

1. Boil the potatoes in salted water for 15 to 20 minutes, or until they are cooked through and tender. Mash the potatoes in a medium bowl.

2. Mix in the butter, egg, salt and flour to form a soft dough. Add more flour, as necessary, to create a smooth, workable dough that is not sticky.

3. Knead the dough on a floured surface. Let it rest for a few minutes.

4. Roll out the dough on a floured surface until it is approximately ⅛ inch thick. Cut into 3-inch squares.

5. In the center of each square, place a plum, ¼ teaspoon sugar and some cinnamon.

6. Fold up the square by bringing opposite corner to opposite corner, and pinch the edges together to form a seal, making the dumpling.

7. To cook the dumplings, drop each one in salted, boiling water. Cook them, 2 or 3 at a time, for 15 minutes.

8. Remove the dumpling with a slotted spoon and place on a serving plate.

9. To make the plum sauce, place the 20 plums in a saucepan with the sugar, cinnamon and water over medium heat. Cook stirring occasionally until a thick sauce is formed and the plums are tender.

Topping:
4 tablespoons (½ stick)
** butter**
½ cup fresh bread crumbs

10. To make the breadcrumb topping, melt the 4 tablespoons of butter in a skillet. Add the bread crumbs, and cook over medium heat, stirring occasionally, for 8 to 10 minutes or until the bread crumbs have browned.

11. Serve the dumplings topped with the plum sauce and the bread crumbs. Add more melted butter, if you wish.

Meat Dumplings Žlinkrofi

Another type of dumpling traditionally served in Slovenia, žlinkrofi are filled with meat. These dumplings can be made with buckwheat or all-purpose flour. The filling can be any leftover meat, but is generally pork or beef and sausages. They may be boiled in salted water, or fried in butter. As are other dumplings, žlinkrofi are served with bread crumbs and melted butter. They can be served as a meal, or as a side dish.

Serves 6 to 8 as a side dish

Dough:
2 cups all-purpose flour
2 eggs, slightly beaten
½ teaspoon salt
1 tablespoon vegetable oil
¼ cup warm water,
  or as needed

Filling:
1½ cups cooked ham or
  other cooked meat,
  ground or cut into small
  pieces
1 or 2 smoked sausages,
  skins removed, ground or
  cut into small pieces
2 eggs, beaten
¼ teaspoon salt, or to taste
¼ cup fresh bread crumbs
2 tablespoons fresh parsley
  or 1 teaspoon dried

Topping:
1 cup fresh bread crumbs
4 tablespoons (½ stick)
  butter

1. To make the dough, in a large bowl combine the flour with the eggs, salt, oil and water. Work the ingredients to form a smooth dough. Add more water if you need to, or add more flour if the dough is sticky.
2. Knead the dough on a floured surface. Place the dough in a greased bowl. Cover and let stand in a warm, protected place for about 1 hour.
3. To prepare the filling, in a medium bowl combine the ham, sausages, eggs, salt, bread crumbs and parsley.
4. To form the dumplings, first roll the dough out on a well-floured surface, or on a floured cloth, until it is ⅛ inch thick.
5. Cut the dough into 3-inch squares.
6. Place a spoonful of the filling into the center of each square. Fold up the squares, bringing opposite corner to opposite corner, and pinch the ends to seal the dough, forming a dumpling.
7. To cook the dumplings, drop 2 or 3 in salted, boiling water for 15 minutes. Or fry the dumplings in a skillet in melted butter for 10 to 12 minutes, until browned.
8. Remove the dumplings with a slotted spoon and place on a serving plate.

9. To make the breadcrumb topping, melt the 4 tablespoons of butter in a skillet. Add the bread crumbs, and cook over medium heat, stirring occasionally, until the bread crumbs have browned.

10. Serve the dumplings topped with the browned bread crumbs. Add more melted butter, if you wish.

Black Risotto *Črni Rižoto*

Black risotto may not sound or look particularly appetizing, but it is a delicious, flavorful dish that is regularly served along the Adriatic Coast. It is risotto made with fresh squid, and its black color comes from the black ink in the squid's ink sacs. Make sure that you use fresh squid and fresh squid ink. This risotto has a great flavor and makes a meal, together with a fresh salad and bread. Or it can be served in small quantities as an appetizer. Make sure to check your teeth after you have eaten it; you don't want to walk away with a black smile! Add other fresh shellfish to this dish, such as shrimp or mussels, if you wish.

Serves 4 as a main meal or 6 as an appetizer

1 pound fresh squid
3 tablespoons olive oil
1 medium onion,
  peeled and chopped
1 to 2 cups white wine
1 to 2 cups water
½ teaspoon salt, or to taste
Freshly ground pepper
Juice of 1 lemon
1 bay leaf
2 cups arborio rice
Freshly grated Parmesan
  cheese, to garnish

1. Cut the squid into slices. Be careful not to puncture the ink sacs. Place the whole ink sacs to the side.

2. In a large skillet, heat the olive oil over medium heat. Add the onion. Cook over medium heat for 8 to 10 minutes, stirring occasionally, until the onion is translucent.

3. Add the squid to the pan. Add ½ cup of wine and ½ cup of water, the salt, pepper to taste, the ink sacs (you may puncture them now), bay leaf and lemon juice.

4. Continue to cook over medium heat for 6 to 8 minutes, or until the squid has softened.

5. Add the rice to the pan and stir. Add another ½ cup of wine and ½ cup of water. Cook for 10 to 12 minutes, stirring continuously, until the rice has absorbed all the liquid.

6. Add another ½ cup of wine and ½ cup of water. Continue to cook over medium heat for another 10 to 12 minutes, stirring continuously, until the rice has absorbed all the liquid.

7. Continue this process, using up all the wine and water, until the rice has cooked all the way through, and is tender. Add more wine and water if you need to. When it is done, there should be a black, creamy sauce with the risotto.

8. Remove the bay leaf. Taste the risotto, and season with salt and pepper as you wish. Serve immediately, sprinkled with fresh Parmesan cheese.

Frutti di Mare Risotto Rižota z Morskimi Sadeži

Despite its Italian sounding name, this is a popular dish in Slovenia. This dish is served along the coast, where fresh shellfish are plentiful. Served with a cold, local white wine or a light red such as a Vipavec or a Koprčan, this dish makes an excellent lunch. Mussels and shrimp are in the recipe, but you may substitute any other fresh shellfish, such as scallops.

Serves 4 as a main dish or 6 as an appetizer

3 tablespoons olive oil
1 medium onion, peeled and chopped
2 cloves garlic, peeled and chopped finely
2 medium tomatoes, chopped
Fresh parsley, cleaned, dried, and chopped
1 teaspoon salt
½ pound fresh mussels
½ pound fresh shrimp
Freshly ground pepper
2 cups arborio rice
2 cups fish stock or water
2 cups white wine
Freshly grated Parmesan cheese, to garnish

1. In a skillet, heat 2 tablespoons oil over medium heat. Add half of the onion, the garlic, tomatoes, parsley, ½ teaspoon of salt, mussels and shrimp. Cook over medium heat for 6 to 8 minutes, stirring continuously, until the shrimp have turned a bright orange. Set aside.

2. In a large skillet, heat 1 tablespoon of the olive oil over medium heat. Add the remaining onion. Cook over medium heat for 8 to 10 minutes, stirring occasionally, until the onion is translucent.

3. Add the rice to the pan. Stir until all of the rice is coated with oil.

4. Add ½ cup of the stock and ½ cup of the wine. Cook, stirring continuously, for 10 to 12 minutes, or until the rice has absorbed all the liquid.

5. Add another ½ cup of stock and ½ cup of wine. Continue to cook over medium heat, stirring continuously, for another 10 to 12 minutes, or until the rice has absorbed all the liquid.

6. Continue to cook the rice mixture, using up all the stock and wine, until the rice has cooked all the way through, and is tender. Add more wine and stock, if you need to.

7. Add the shellfish mixture to the rice. Heat through. Season the risotto with salt and freshly ground pepper. Serve hot, sprinkled with freshly grated Parmesan cheese.

Mushroom Risotto Gobova Rižota

Serve this risotto with a dry white wine, such as a Laski Rizling or a Ljutomerčan.

Serves 4 as a side dish

2 tablespoons butter or
   olive oil
2 cups mushrooms (wild or
   cultivated), washed, dried
   and sliced
½ cup fresh parsley,
   washed, dried, and
   chopped
1 medium onion,
   peeled and chopped
1 cup arborio rice
2 to 3 cups chicken stock
1 to 2 cups white wine
2 teaspoons fresh
   marjoram or 1 teaspoon
   dried
½ cup freshly grated
   Parmesan cheese
Salt
Freshly ground pepper

1. In a small to medium skillet, heat half of the butter or oil over medium heat. Add the mushrooms and parsley. Cook over medium heat, stirring occasionally, for 12 to 15 minutes, or until the mushrooms are tender and all the liquid has evaporated from the pan.
2. Remove the mushrooms from the heat.
3. In a large skillet, heat the rest of the oil. Add the onion. Cook over medium heat for 8 to 10 minutes, stirring continuously, until translucent.
4. Add the rice to the pan. Stir until the rice has been coated with the onion mixture.
5. Add 1 cup of the stock, ½ cup of the wine and the marjoram. Cook over medium heat, stirring continuously, for 10 to 12 minutes, or until the rice has absorbed all of the liquid.
6. Add another cup of stock and ½ cup of wine. Cook, stirring continuously, for another 10 to 12 minutes, until the rice has absorbed all of the liquid.
7. Continue cooking the rice in this way until the rice has cooked all the way through. Add more stock and water, if necessary. There should be a creamy sauce with the rice.
8. Add the mushroom mixture. Stir in the Parmesan cheese. Season the risotto with salt and pepper, to taste. Serve hot, sprinkled with a bit of fresh parsley.

Istrian Pasta Fuži

Fuži is a type of pasta which is popular in southeastern Slovenia and in Istria, the peninsula that is now Croatia. Over the years, the border of Istria, between Slovenia, Croatia, and Italy, has changed many times. In fact, many city signs are trilingual, written in the now-native Slovenian, Croatian, and Italian. This homemade pasta is almost like a penne. It can be served with butter as a side dish, or with your favorite sauce or goulash.

**Serves 4 as a main dish
or 6 as an appetizer**

**3½ cups all-purpose flour
2 eggs, slightly beaten
2 tablespoons oil
1 tablespoon white wine
1 teaspoon salt, or to taste**

1. In a large bowl, put the flour and make a well in the center.
2. In the well, place the eggs, oil, white wine and salt. Mix the ingredients to form a workable dough. Add more flour, if the dough is sticky, or more wine, if the dough is too dry.
3. On a floured surface, knead the dough for ten minutes. Roll the dough out on a lightly floured surface, to a thickness of ⅛ inch. Cut the dough into 1-inch strips. Cut the strips into pieces that are 1 inch long.
4. Shape each piece of dough around your finger or the handle of a large wooden spoon, by taking two opposing corners and bringing them together to touch each other.
5. As you form them, place the pasta on a floured surface or cookie sheet. Allow them to dry for about 30 minutes.
6. To cook the pasta, place them in boiling, salted water for 3 to 5 minutes, or until the pasta is tender.
7. Drain and serve hot with melted butter, any pasta sauce or goulash.

Pasta with Beans Pašta Fižol

This is another recipe from the Primorska region of Slovenia, which forms the Western border of Slovenia with Italy. In Italian, this dish is called pasta e fagiole.

Serves 6

2 pounds dried kidney beans, soaked in cold water for at least 4 hours, or overnight
3 tablespoons olive oil
¼ pound dried pork, or 3 or 4 slices bacon, cut into small pieces
1 small onion, peeled and chopped
½ cup all-purpose flour
¼ cup tomato puree
2 cloves garlic, peeled and minced
2 teaspoons fresh marjoram or 1 teaspoon dried
1 bay leaf
½ teaspoon salt, or to taste
Freshly ground pepper
1½ pounds short, fat pasta such as penne or macaroni
Splash of vinegar

1. Place the beans in a large saucepan, and fill with enough salted water to cover the beans. Bring to a boil. Reduce the heat and let the beans simmer over medium heat for 1 hour, or until they are tender. Do not drain.
2. In a skillet, heat the olive oil over medium heat. Add the meat, and cook over medium heat for a few minutes. Add the onion, and continue to cook, stirring occasionally, for 5 to 8 minutes, or until the onion is translucent.
3. Add the flour, tomato puree, and garlic to the meat and onion mixture.
4. Add a few tablespoons of water, and stir. Continue to cook for 10 to 12 minutes, or until a smooth sauce has formed. Add more water if necessary.
5. Add the meat mixture to the beans. Add the marjoram, bay leaf, salt and pepper. Cook over medium heat until the sauce is quite thick, another 8 to 10 minutes.
6. In the meantime, cook the pasta in salted, boiling water for 8 to 10 minutes, or until it is tender. Drain and rinse with cold water.
7. Add a splash of vinegar to the meat and bean sauce. Remove the bay leaf before serving. Serve the pasta covered with the sauce.

Pasta with Pumpkin Sauce Rezanci z Bučo

This is a great fall pasta dish. If you can't find fresh pumpkin, you may substitute another orange squash or gourd.

Serves 4

3 tablespoons butter
2 shallots, peeled and
  chopped
1 pound pumpkin or
  winter squash, such as
  butternut, peeled,
  seeded, and cut into
  small chunks
½ cup dry white wine
1 to 2 cups chicken broth
½ teaspoon ground
  nutmeg
½ teaspoon salt, or to taste
Freshly ground pepper
½ pound long, flat noodles
  such as tagliatelle
½ cup grated Parmesan
  cheese

1. In a large skillet, melt the butter over medium heat. Add the shallots. Cook the shallots over medium heat for 6 to 8 minutes, or until they are translucent. Add the pumpkin, white wine and chicken broth. Let simmer over medium heat until the pumpkin is cooked all the way through (about 30 minutes).

2. If you would like to make a smooth sauce, mash the pumpkin with a potato masher, or process in a food processor; or leave it chunky.

3. Flavor the sauce with the nutmeg, salt and pepper.

4. Cook the pasta in boiling salted water until tender. Drain.

5. Serve the pasta with the sauce. Sprinkle with Parmesan cheese.

BLED

Here to this isle with lake encircling
   round
Which nowadays is Mary's holy shrine:
Against the sky stand tow'ring peaks
   snowbound,
Before them spread the fields; the fair outline
Of Castle Bled perfects the left foreground,
While rolling hills the right hand side define.
No, Carniola has no prettier scene
Than this, resembling paradise serene.

– France Prešeren, from
"The Baptism on the Savica."
Translated by Tom Priestly and
Henry Cooper

Curling on Lake Bled, ca 1929.

In his epic poem, "The Baptism on the Savica," France Prešeren, Slovenia's national poet, describes the most picturesque town in Slovenia. Located on Lake Bled, with its island chapel, medieval castle on the cliff above, surrounded by the highest peaks of the Julian Alps and the Karavanke, Bled is truly spectacular. Bled has also been a symbol of Slovenian nationalism for centuries.

Bled was the site of a Hallstatt settlement in the early Iron Age, but was out of the way for major trade routes, and the Romans didn't pay much attention to it. In the seventh century, Slavs were attracted to the valley by its mild climate and the natural protection provided by the surrounding mountains. Bled has been linked to Slavic legends and myths ever since, especially the ancient Slavic goddess Živa. In 1004, the German emperor Henry II presented Bled Castle and its lands to the bishops of Brixen in south Tirol. It remained under the Brixen rule until it was taken over by the Habsburgs in the early nineteenth century.

Bled became well known as a spa town. Pilgrims who visited to pray at the chapel on the island in Lake Bled had always been familiar with its healing warm waters and natural springs. The beauty and warm waters of Bled were described in Janez Vajkard Valvasor's *The Glory of the Duchy of Carniola*, written in 1689. In the late eighteenth century, the keeper of the castle seriously considered draining Lake Bled, to use the clay for making bricks. Fortunately, a Swiss doctor came along who fully appreciated all that Bled had to offer. Arnold Rikli opened baths in 1855, setting up a spa where he practiced his own school of healing and natural medicine

(see "Arnold Rikli: Sunshine Salesman," page 121). A railway opened in 1870 between Ljubljana and Tarvisio, and Bled became a popular vacation spot for wealthy Europeans right up until World War II. Bled was the summer residence of the Karadžordževići, the Yugoslav royal family. Their villa was destroyed in 1938. Josip Broz Tito was also known to spend time here, recuperating and enjoying his summers at the hotel Vila Bled.

Bled has many tourist attractions, including Bled Castle (see "The Country of Castles," page 203). Bled Island is the only island in Slovenia and has always been a place of worship, going back to early Slavs who worshipped at a pagan temple here. Today, there stands the Baroque Church of the Assumption, dating back to the ninth century. It is a popular place for weddings. The chapel is approached by a large staircase that was built in 1655. It is said that the groom must carry the bride up these ninety-nine steps for the couple to have good fortune. There is also a bell, which can be rung if you would like to make a wish. The six-kilometer walk around Lake Bled is quite pleasant. At one time, there were many grand villas and hotels around Lake Bled. One of the few that remain today is the Grand Hotel Toplice, right on the shores of Lake Bled, built in 1850. The natural springs the lake had to offer were always a draw to this beautiful turn-of-the-century hotel, and the hotel pool is still filled from the springs every morning.

Besides being a wonderful place to rest and relax, Bled has many activities to offer. There is skiing at nearby Vogel Mountain, golf at Bled Golf and Country Club, some of the best hiking in Central Europe, and rowing on Lake Bled. Whitewater rafting, fishing, biking, and paragliding are all offered in the surrounding area.

The elegant logo of the Grand Hotel Toplice, Bled.

Lithograph depicting Bled by Jožef Wagner, 1942.

THE LEGEND OF THE BIRTH OF LAKE BLED

Legend has it that Lake Bled was created when God became angry with the people of Bled for allowing their animals to graze around Mary's church, despite God's warning to build a fence. The animals even wandered inside the church. Because the people wouldn't listen to him, God created Lake Bled as a natural barrier to the place of worship.

An old poster, ca 1938, promotes tourism in Bled.

THE LEGEND OF ERAZEM LUEGER:
A SLOVENIAN ROBIN HOOD

As depicted by writer and Renaissance man Janez Vajkard Valvasor, Erazem Lueger was a Slovenian Robin Hood, stealing from the rich and giving to the poor. During the wars between the Austrians and the Hungarians in the fifteenth century, Lueger supported the Hungarians against the evil Austrian king Frederick III. In the fall of 1483, the Hungarians were holed up in Predjama Castle, while the Austrians attacked for months at a time. Unable to penetrate the castle, the Austrians were confused as to how the inhabitants were able to survive, with apparently no access to food or drink. It turned out that Lueger regularly escaped from the castle through a secret passageway that was hidden by a rock. He came and went as he pleased, continuing his thieving ways as well as providing fresh food and water to the Hungarian troops in the castle. He enjoyed taunting the Austrians by throwing fresh fish and fruit at them. King Frederick became angry and Lueger became a target for the Austrians. One day, while sitting in the water closet, he was hit by an Austrian cannonball. Apparently a servant betrayed him, and raised a flag marking the location of the water closet, making it easy for the Austrians to get their man.

Voda seveda koristi, še več
zrak in največ svetloba.
Water of course is good,
air even better,
but light is the best.

– Arnold Rikli

ARNOLD RIKLI: SUNSHINE SALESMAN

Arnold Rikli, called "the sunny doctor" or "the crazy doctor," had his own prescription for healing, which included fresh air, sunshine, and exercise. Although he was controversial in his day, the National Medicine Institute that he established in Bled in 1855 helped create international recognition for Bled as a spa and resort town. Taking advantage of all that Lake Bled and the surrounding mountains had to offer in such a natural and unobtrusive manner established Rikli as a Slovenian hero.

Rikli was born in Wagen, Switzerland, in 1823. Although technically trained in medicine, he had always been interested in natural healing methods. When he was recovering from his own ailments, someone recommended that he visit Bled. He did so in 1854, and was so impressed he decided to stay. His Natural Medicine Institute included fifty-six airy huts along Lake Bled, and a central building with a modest dining room where vegetarian meals were served. He routinely prescribed fresh air and sunshine, recommending "air baths" even in the cold of winter. He also stressed the importance of exercise, and his patients took long walks and hikes, and went swimming in Lake Bled every day. He also simplified his patients' diet, serving vegetarian fare. Sleeping outside and nudism were also practiced by the "Riklies." Rikli was known to practice his own methods routinely.

Rikli hated traditional medicine, and was often critical of its methods. He was controversial, and many thought him crazy for "selling" fresh air, sunshine, and nudism. He published several books, and one of them was even banned in 1900. He was brought to court for his open criticism of the traditional medical field many times. However, Rikli also had many supporters, and his patients were grateful to him for curing their depression, insomnia, dysentery, and many other ailments. He also had many imitators who built similar spas in Bled, Germany, and Switzerland. Rikli is now praised as one of the most important natural healers of the second half of the nineteenth century. His major anniversaries are celebrated, and Germany and Switzerland celebrate him as a great inventor, annually passing out Rikli medals and prizes.

THE GHOST OF MOKRICE CASTLE

It is said that Mokrice Castle is haunted by the ghost of a seventeenth century countess named Barbara. Barbara fell in love with a sailor named Marko, well below her in social rank. Marko left for the sea, and failed to return. Barbara was so heartbroken that she took her own life. Her ghost roams the stairways and secret passageways of the castle at night. It is believed, she is particularly active on the celebrated feast day of Saint Barbara, her namesake's day, December 4.

SLOVENIANS' LOVE OF THE OUTDOORS

Slovenians have a strong attachment to nature, and most of them lead very active, outdoor lives. Not only is Slovenia rich in natural beauty, but there are also many opportunities to enjoy the outdoors that all families can enjoy.

Skiing has a long history in Slovenia, and more than 300,000 Slovenians enjoy the sport. The first written record of the sport in the seventeenth century refers to skiing on the Bloke Plateau, in the region of Notranjska. Although Slovenia does not have the highest peaks in Europe, there are many beautiful, and affordable, resorts to enjoy. The largest ski resorts are Mariborsko Pohorje, in the northeast corner of the country, and in Koranjska Gora. There is also a small resort at Mount Vogel at Lake Bohinj. Snowboarding, cross-country skiing, and ski jumping are also popular in Slovenia. Slovenia hosts international ski-jumping and ski-flying competitions, and the Slovenian national team has won many cross-country and biathlon events.

Slovenia also offers a wonderful system of hiking trails, and many Slovenians enjoy hiking and walking in the woods and the mountains. Rock climbing, mountaineering, and cycling are also very popular, especially in the area of Triglav. Kayaking, canoeing, and rafting are available on local rivers. Sailing and windsurfing are popular not only off the coast at Portorož, but also on Lake Bohinj. Fishing is a common sport, especially for freshwater trout. And Slovenia is known with horseback riders as the home of the famous "Lipizzaner" horses, bred in the Slovenian town of Lipica. There are several beautiful golf courses in Slovenia (see "Playing Golf in Slovenia," page 62), and tennis courts, chessboards, basketball courts are to be found in the outdoors.

Spa resorts are very common in Slovenia, which is known for its natural springs. There are sixteen thermal spa resorts in the country, steam rooms, "cures," and other ways to relax. Some of them, such as the Dolenjske Toplice, have real turn-of-the-century charm. Many others, such as the Čatež Terme, near Mokrice Castle, have more of a communal feel, with large pools and changing rooms that can accommodate many people. Some of the spas, such as the Banovci spa, are for "naturists." Spas are enjoyed in both the winter and summer months. They can be very relaxing, especially if one has spent the whole day enjoying the outdoors!

Meat, Fish, and Game

Če se ya novega leta ne naješ,
boš vse leto lačen.
Eat plenty at New Year,
or go hungry all year long.

– Slovenian proverb

Goulash Golaž

It is not unusual to see goulash on German, Austrian, Hungarian, and Slovenian menus. Found more often in mountainous regions, golaž is a tasty way to serve combinations of meat, such as veal, beef, and venison. Especially in the winter months, a warm bowl of goulash that has been cooking for hours will warm you up after a long day outside. It can be served as a soup, or as a main meal. At the top of Mount Vogel, near Lake Bohinj in northern Slovenia, the Alpine hut Planinska koča Merjasec (Wild Boar Lodge) serves wild boar goulash over polenta to skiers and hikers. This recipe is typical in that it includes chunks of meat and paprika, the latter a staple of the Austro-Hungarian Empire that once dominated the region.

Serves 4 to 6

3 to 4 tablespoons lard or
  butter
3 medium onions,
  peeled and chopped
2 small cloves garlic,
  peeled and minced
¼ teaspoon ground cumin
1 teaspoon salt
½ teaspoon freshly ground
  pepper
1 teaspoon paprika
1 teaspoon dried marjoram
1 pound veal, cut into
  cubes
1 pound beef, or other
  meat, cut into cubes
2 tablespoons all-purpose
  flour
2 cups beef broth or water
½ cup red wine

1. In a skillet, melt the butter or lard over medium heat. Add the onions, and continue to cook over medium heat for 5 to 6 minutes, stirring occasionally. Add the garlic, cumin, salt, pepper, paprika and marjoram. Stir well. Cook for another 2 to 3 minutes, or until the onions are translucent and slightly browned.
2. Add the meat and the 2 tablespoons flour. Cook over medium to high heat, stirring continuously, until the beef is browned on all sides, about 8 to 10 minutes.
3. Once the beef is browned, add the broth. The liquid should just cover all of the meat. Cover and cook over low to medium heat for 1 to 2 hours. Check the sauce, if it is watery, cook the goulash uncovered for the last half hour.
4. Just before serving, stir in the red wine. Heat through.
5. The goulash is ready to serve! Serve with potatoes, polenta, dumplings, or simply with fresh, crusty bread.

Turkey Fillets with Gorgonzola Sauce Puranji Zrezek v Gorgonzolevi Omaki

In Slovenia, it is more common to see turkey than chicken on the menu. This recipe is a favorite at Gostilna pri Planincu in Bled. Served with roasted potatoes, it is a flavorful, filling dish.

Serves 6

Turkey:
6 turkey or chicken fillets (about 1½ pounds)
3 tablespoons all-purpose flour
3 tablespoons olive oil or butter
2 cloves garlic, peeled and minced

Gorgonzola Sauce:
2 tablespoons butter
½ pound Gorgonzola cheese, crumbled
½ to 1 cup cream
½ teaspoon freshly ground pepper, or to taste

1. Pound the turkey fillets until they are tenderized. Coat the fillets with flour.
2. In a skillet, heat the olive oil or butter. Add the garlic and cook for 2 to 3 minutes over medium heat.
3. Add the turkey fillets to the pan. Cook over medium to high heat for 10 to 12 minutes, or until the fillets are nicely browned on the outside, and the meat is cooked through.
4. To make the sauce, melt the butter in a saucepan. Add the Gorgonzola cheese and cream. Cook over low to medium heat, stirring occasionally, for 3 to 4 minutes, or until the cheese has melted. The sauce should be slightly thick. Add more cream if you need to. Season to taste with the freshly ground pepper.
5. Serve the fillets covered with the Gorgonzola sauce and garnished with parsley or grated Parmesan cheese.

Roast Turkey with Traditional Flour Noodles Pečen Puran z Mlinci

This is a very traditional dish in Slovenia. Mlinci *is a flour-based flat noodle of sorts, which is often served with turkey, rabbit, or duck. It is a simple addition to the meal and because it is a dry noodle, nicely soaks up the juices of the meat.*

Serves 6

Stuffing:
3 to 4 tablespoons butter or oil
1 turkey liver or 2 to 3 chicken livers, cut into small pieces
¼ pound sausages, cut into small pieces
1 medium onion, peeled and chopped
2 garlic cloves, peeled and minced
½ teaspoon salt
Freshly ground pepper
2 teaspoons fresh marjoram or 2 teaspoons dried
2 cups fresh bread crumbs
2 cups chestnuts, roasted, peeled and pureed (optional) (see page 99 for how to roast and peel chestnuts)

1. To prepare the stuffing, in a large pan, heat the butter over medium heat. Add the liver, sausages, onion and garlic, salt and pepper and marjoram. Cook for 10 to 15 minutes over medium heat, stirring continuously, until the onions are nicely browned.

2. Add the bread crumbs. Add the chestnuts to this mixture, if you wish. Mix well. Let the stuffing cool.

3. Clean the turkey. Stuff the inside of the turkey with the stuffing.

4. Place the turkey in a roasting pan. Brush the turkey with the melted butter. Roast at 375°F for 3 hours, or until the turkey is cooked all the way through, and the skin is nicely browned, basting the meat with its own juices every 20 minutes. After the first hour, add the water or chicken stock.

5. While the turkey roasts, prepare the mlinci. Make a dough with the flour, water, egg and salt. If the dough is too sticky, you may add more flour. If the dough is too dry, you may add more water.

6. Divide the dough into 3 pieces. On a lightly floured surface, knead each piece of dough for 10 minutes. Allow each piece of dough to rest for about 1 hour.

7. Roll each piece of dough out onto a floured surface, until it is ½ to ¾ inch thick.

Turkey:
1 small turkey
 (6 to 8 pounds)
¼ pound (1 stick) butter,
 melted
2 to 3 cups chicken or
 turkey stock, or water
1 teaspoon salt

Mlinci:
3 cups all-purpose flour
1 cup water
1 egg
½ teaspoon salt

8. Place on a greased baking sheet. Bake the mlinci at 350°F for 15 to 20 minutes, or until it is firm, and slightly browned at the edges. (If you only have one oven, you may bake the mlinci with the turkey at 375°F, just keep a close eye on it to make sure you don't over-cook it.)

9. Take the mlinci out of the oven and let cool. Right before using the mlinci, break it into pieces, or cut it into strips. Pour boiling water over the mlinci, and let it sit for a few minutes, then drain.

10. Towards the end of the cooking of the turkey, add the mlinci to the pan. Allow the mlinci to cook in the pan with the turkey for at least 15 minutes.

11. Once the turkey meat is cooked through, remove the bird from the oven. Slice the meat. Serve the turkey with the stuffing, surrounded by the mlinci, and topped with the juices from the pan.

A modern design by Klemen Rodman of the Heavenly Peacock found in archeological digs in Slovenia. As a pagan symbol, the peacock represented immortality, eternal life, and never-ending spring. As a Christian symbol, the bird's triangular beak symbolizes the Holy Trinity.

St. Martin's Roast Goose Martinova Pečena Gos

St. Martin's Day is November 11. Although not a public holiday, it is an important day in Slovenia, as this is the day that the winemakers' must (fermenting grape juice) officially becomes wine, and can be sold as such. People celebrate with this goose dish served with young wine and accompanied by folk music played in local restaurants.

Serves 6

Goose:
1 teaspoon salt
½ teaspoon ground pepper
1 teaspoon dried marjoram
1 tablespoon caraway seeds, crushed
1 goose (about 5 pounds)
3 tablespoons butter or oil
3 or 4 shallots, or 2 medium onions, peeled and chopped
4 medium apples, peeled, cored, and sliced
½ pound chestnuts, cooked, peeled, and finely chopped (see page 99 for how to cook and peel chestnuts)
½ cup wine
3 tablespoons brandy

Mlinci:
1 recipe mlinci (see pages 130-131, steps 5 to 9)

1. Combine the salt, pepper, marjoram, and caraway seeds. Rub the inside and outside of the goose with this mixture.

2. Heat the oil or butter in a small pan. Add the shallots or onions and cook over medium heat until they are slightly browned.

3. Combine the apples and chestnuts with the cooked shallots. Stuff the inside of the goose with this mixture.

4. Place the goose in a roasting dish, and pour the wine over it.

5. Roast at 400°F for 1½ hours. Baste every 15 minutes with the juices from the goose. Keep an eye on the bird to make sure that it doesn't brown too quickly. If it browns too quickly, cover the bird with tinfoil while it continues to cook.

6. Just before the goose is ready to take out of the oven, coat it with the brandy.

7. When the goose has a nice brown crust and is tender on the inside, it is done.

8. Remove it from the oven and remove the goose from the pan.

9. Add the mlinci to the pan and return to the oven for 5 to 10 minutes.

10. Serve the goose with its own juices, mlinci, roast potatoes, or dumplings, and vegetables such as cabbage.

Partridge from the Prekmurje Region of Slovenia Prekmurska Jerebica

This partridge recipe comes from the Prekmurje region of Slovenia, the northeast corner of the country that borders Hungary. Partridge may be hard to come by in some areas. You may substitute chicken, Cornish game hen, or duck; however, partridge has a unique flavor that you will be missing. You will need to marinate the partridge 3 to 4 days before cooking it.

Serves 4 to 6

Marinade:
2 carrots, peeled and
  chopped
1 parsnip, chopped
1 small onion, peeled and
  chopped
1 garlic clove,
  peeled and minced
3 tablespoons juniper
  berries, cranberries or
  currants, crushed
½ teaspoon salt
Freshly ground pepper

Partridge:
1 partridge
3 slices bacon
1 medium onion,
  peeled and chopped
2 cloves garlic, peeled and
  minced
1 tablespoon all-purpose
  flour
1 cup chicken stock
½ teaspoon ground cumin
3 tablespoons chopped
  fresh parsley
2 teaspoons sweet paprika
1 cup sour cream

1. To prepare the marinade, combine the carrots, parsnip, onion, garlic, juniper berries, salt and pepper. Coat the partridge with the marinade. Cover tightly and marinate in the refrigerator for 3 to 4 days.

2. Remove the partridge from the marinade. Wrap one piece of the bacon around the partridge. Brush the bird with oil or melted butter. Place in a roasting dish, and cover it. Roast in the oven at 375°F for 30 to 40 minutes, until the bird is tender and the skin is nicely browned. Baste with its own juices every 15 to 20 minutes.

3. Cut the remaining bacon into small pieces. For the last 15 minutes in the oven, add the bacon, onion, garlic and flour to the roasting pan with the partridge.

4. Remove the partridge from the pan, and keep it warm. To the roasting pan, add the chicken stock, cumin, parsley and paprika. Return to the oven for a few minutes, until the sauce begins to simmer.

5. Remove the pan from the oven. Stir in the sour cream. Season the sauce as you wish.

6. Serve the partridge with the sauce and mlinci.

Roast Duck Kvinta

The origin of the name of this recipe, kvinta, *is the Latin word for "one hundred." In Slovenia, it is traditionally thought that 100-day-old ducks are the best for roasting. Duck is often served during the Christmas holidays.*

Serves 6

Duck:
1 small (6 to 8 pounds) duck (preferably 100 days old)
1 tablespoon salt
4 tablespoons butter, oil or lard

Stuffing:
1 pound chestnuts, cooked and peeled (see page 99 for how to peel chestnuts), or 2 cups fresh bread crumbs
3 or 4 slices bacon, cut into small pieces
½ cup white wine
½ teaspoon salt
Freshly ground pepper
2 tablespoons fresh rosemary, or 2 teaspoons dried
3 apples, peeled, cored, and chopped

Mlinci:
1 recipe mlinci (see pages 130-131, steps 5 to 9)

1. To make the stuffing, cut the cooked and peeled chestnuts into small pieces, or process them in a food processor.
2. Combine the chestnuts with the bacon, white wine, salt, pepper, rosemary and apples.
3. Clean the duck. Rub it on the inside and outside with salt.
4. Stuff the inside of the duck with the stuffing.
5. Brush the top of the duck with the oil or melted butter.
6. Place the duck in a roasting pan, and roast at 425°F for 2 hours. Keep an eye on the duck. It should brown nicely. Baste it occasionally with its own juices. If necessary, add water to the pan to help create more juice.
7. When the duck is tender and browned, remove from the oven.
8. Remove the duck from the pan, and keep warm.
9. Place the mlinci in the pan, and return to the oven for 5 to 10 minutes.
10. Slice the duck. Serve with the mlinci and its own juices.

Pig on a Spit Prašiček Pečen na Ražnju

Roasting a whole pig is a tradition in many cultures. The slowly roasted, tender meat is often enjoyed in the summertime, when outdoor grills can be used. An indoor grill may also be used in the cooler weather. Throughout Slovenia, whole roasted pig can be enjoyed in people's homes, or at roadside inns, where the meat is served by the kilo.

Serves 25 to 30

1 whole pig (it is important that the head of the pig is still attached)
½ to 1 cup salt
½ cup pepper
7 or 8 cloves garlic, peeled and minced
3 or 4 apples (optional)
3 or 4 medium onions, peeled (optional)

1. Clean the pig thoroughly with water and pat dry.
2. Combine the salt, pepper and garlic. Rub mixture on the inside and outside of the pig. If you wish, you may stuff the cavity of the pig with the apples and the onions.
3. Spit the pig by piercing it with a stainless steel rod (the spit). Make sure that the pig is attached to the spit at 3 or 4 spots along the length of the pig. It is important that the head of the pig is firmly attached to one end of the spit. Also make sure that the meat of the pig is stretched along the spit, so that the meat cooks evenly.
4. Set the spit with the pig on a strong and secure stand approximately 3 to 4 feet above a controlled fire. Prop the spit so that you may easily turn it, rotating the pig continually.
5. Roast the pig over a low flame for 3 to 4 hours, turning the pig slowly at all times, until the meat is tender. A hard wood is best to use for the fire, such as hickory or oak. Watch it carefully, to make sure that the fat dripping into the fire does not create too high flames.
6. If the pig becomes brown on the outside, you may cover with tinfoil to make sure that it does not burn.
7. When the pig is done, the meat will be very tender. It is best to have several hands available to remove the pig from the spit.
8. Carve and serve. Delicious!

Leg of Pork Stuffed with Dried Figs
Nadevana Svinjska Ribica s Suhimi Figami

The sweet and juicy figs provide a great complement to the pork in this popular Slovenian dish.

Serves 4

1 pork leg (3 to 4 pounds)
1 teaspoon salt
½ teaspoon freshly ground pepper
4 tablespoons (½ stick) butter
2 shallots or 1 small onion, peeled and chopped
¼ pound dried figs (about 1½ cups), coarsely chopped
1 cup white wine
1 tablespoon fresh rosemary or 1 teaspoon dried
2 or 3 tablespoons plum or other fruit brandy or white wine
1 tablespoon prepared mustard
1 cup cream

1. Clean and bone the pork, and make a large steak from it. Tenderize the meat by pounding it, and season with salt and pepper.
2. In a skillet, melt 2 tablespoons of butter. Add the shallots or onion, and cook over medium heat for 5 to 6 minutes, stirring continuously.
3. Add 1 cup of the figs and ½ cup white wine to the shallots. Add the rosemary. Continue to cook and stir until the shallots are tender, and some of the liquid has evaporated, another 3 to 4 minutes.
4. Spread the shallot and fig mixture evenly over the pork steak.
5. Roll the pork tightly and tie with a string.
6. Place the pork in a roasting pan. Dot the outside of the pork with 2 tablespoons of butter. Season with salt and pepper, if you wish. Sprinkle with the remaining figs.
7. Roast the pork at 325°F for approximately 1 hour. Every 10 to 15 minutes, baste the pork with its own juices. If necessary, add water or wine to the pan to create more juice.
8. When the pork is tender and nicely browned on the outside, remove it from the oven. Remove the meat from the pan, and keep warm.
9. To make the sauce, pour the juices from the pan into a skillet. Add the remaining ½ cup white wine, the plum brandy and mustard. Cook over medium heat, stirring continuously, for 6 to 8 minutes.

10. Stir in the cream. Remove the sauce from heat.

11. Slice the pork and serve with the sauce and potatoes or noodles.

Roast Leg of Lamb Pečena Ovčja Bedra

It is said that the best meat for roasting comes from a six-week-old lamb. This dish is often served in the spring.

Serves 8

2 cloves garlic, peeled and crushed
1 teaspoon salt
1 teaspoon pepper
1 leg of lamb, about 5 pounds
2 cloves garlic, peeled and sliced thickly, optional
4 sprigs fresh rosemary
4 tablespoons oil or butter, melted

1. Combine the crushed garlic, salt, and pepper.

2. Clean the lamb. Rub the salt and garlic mixture into the meat. Allow to rest for 1 hour.

3. Cut several slits into the meat. Place the thick slices of garlic into the slits, if you wish.

4. Place the leg of lamb in a roasting pan. Drizzle with the oil or melted butter and surround with the rosemary sprigs.

5. Roast at 325°F for approximately 2 to 2½ hours. Baste every 20 minutes with the juices from the lamb. Add water to the pan, if necessary, to create more juice.

6. Make sure that the lamb does not brown too quickly. If it does, you may turn down the heat to 300°F, or cover with tinfoil while it continues to cook.

7. When the meat is tender and the outside of the lamb is nicely browned, the lamb is done.

8. Serve with roasted potatoes and cooked vegetables.

Venison Bohinj Style Divjačina po Bohinsjsko

This recipe is from the area of Lake Bohinj, in the Gorenjska region of Slovenia. Here in the Julian Alps, another source of sustenance for the local population has traditionally been, and remains today, hunting. Red and roe deer are still in abundance in these mountains, and venison can often be found on local menus, especially in the fall.

Serves 6 to 8

1 venison leg (about 4½
   pounds)
¼ pound bacon
1 teaspoon salt, or to taste
2 cups chopped mixed
   fresh vegetables: carrots,
   celery, and onions
   (add parsley, if desired)
3 tablespoons bacon fat
   or butter
2 tablespoons peppercorns,
   or to taste
2 tablespoons juniper
   berries, or to taste
3 or 4 sprigs fresh
   rosemary
2 cups broth or water
½ cup sour cream
⅓ cup dried cranberries
2 teaspoons vinegar

1. Clean the venison meat, cutting away fat and removing any bones.

2. Wrap the meat with several strips of bacon and season with salt.

3. Chop the remaining bacon into small pieces. Place the chopped bacon in a large skillet. Add the chopped fresh vegetables, bacon fat or butter, peppercorns, juniper berries, and rosemary.

4. Cook the vegetables over medium heat for 12 to 15 minutes, stirring occasionally. When the vegetables are tender, remove them from the heat.

5. Place the vegetables in the bottom of a large roasting pan. Place the venison on top of the vegetables.

6. Preheat the oven to 375°F. Place the roasting pan in the oven.

7. Roast the meat for 45 minutes to 1 hour, or until the meat has browned.

8. Add the broth to the pan. Baste the meat with the juices that form at the bottom of the pan.

9. Continue cooking the meat for another 30 to 40 minutes, until it is tender, basting every 10 minutes. If you prefer rare meat, cook it a shorter period. If you prefer well-done meat, cook it longer. Cut into the center of the venison to check on the color of the meat, to determine how cooked it is.

10. Once the meat is close to being ready, stir the sour cream and cranberries into the juices in the pan. Continue to roast the venison for a few more minutes.

11. Remove the meat from the oven when it is cooked to your preference.

12. Add a dash of vinegar to the sauce in the pan. Stir the sauce, and serve it with the meat.

13. Slice the meat thinly and serve with roasted potatoes and cranberry sauce (see recipe page 212).

Roast Venison Dušena Srna

This recipe comes from Marina Kristanc, the head chef at the Grand Hotel Toplice in Bled.

Serves 6 to 8

1 venison leg (about 4½ pounds)

Marinade:
1 medium onion, peeled and chopped
2 carrots, peeled and sliced
2 stalks celery, cleaned and chopped
2 sprigs rosemary
1 tablespoon juniper berries or currants, crushed
2 tablespoons chopped fresh parsley
1 teaspoon salt

Sauce:
3 tablespoons butter or oil
2 tablespoons all-purpose flour
1 cup tomato puree
½ cup red wine

1. Clean the venison.
2. Combine the onion, carrots, celery, rosemary, berries, parsley and salt. Rub the venison with the marinade. Allow to marinate, covered and refrigerated, for 1 to 2 days.
3. Remove the venison from the marinade, reserving marinade. In a large saucepan, heat half of the oil or butter. Quickly brown the venison on each side over medium to high heat. Place the venison in a roasting dish.
4. In a saucepan, heat the remaining butter or oil. Place the marinade into the pan. Cook over medium heat, stirring frequently, for 3 to 4 minutes.
5. Add the flour, tomato puree and red wine. Stir and continue to cook for another 3 to 4 minutes.
6. Pour the sauce over the venison. Roast the venison at 400°F for 1½ hours, covered, or until the meat is tender and the sauce is browned. While the venison is roasting, baste it with its own juices. If you run low on liquid, you may add more wine or water to the pan.
7. Remove the venison from the oven. Slice it and serve with the gravy, dumplings or potatoes, and cranberry sauce (see recipe page 212).

Stuffed Veal Chops Polnjen Telečji Kotlet

One of the nicest hotels in Bled is Hotel Vila Bled, where General Tito, the long-time ruler of the former Yugoslavia, used to stay while he vacationed in Bled. This recipe has been translated by the hotel's general manager, Janez Fajfar.

½ pound calf's liver

1 medium onion, peeled and finely chopped

2 garlic cloves, peeled and crushed

½ teaspoon freshly ground pepper

⅓ cup fresh bread crumbs

2 tablespoons chopped fresh parsley

Rind of 1 lemon, grated

4 veal chops (about 2 pounds)

3 tablespoons oil or butter, melted

1 cup water or beef broth, or as needed

1. Finely chop the liver. In a bowl, combine the liver with the onion, garlic, pepper, bread crumbs, parsley and lemon rind.

2. Cut a slit horizontally into the center of each veal chop. Stuff each slit with the liver mixture. Pack them as tightly as you can.

3. Place the chops in a baking dish. (If you have extra stuffing left over, you may sprinkle it over the meat.)

4. Drizzle the oil or melted butter over the meat.

5. Roast the veal chops at 400°F for 35 to 40 minutes. Baste the chops with their own juices every 5 to 10 minutes. If there is no liquid to baste with, then add water or broth to the pan.

6. When the chops are tender and slightly browned at the edges, they are done. Be careful not to overcook them, otherwise they will be dry.

7. Serve the veal chops with their own juices and potatoes or risotto.

Cabbage Rolls *Sarma*

Sarma (kohlrouladen in German, głombki in Polish), a tasty dish made of cabbage and meat, has many variations in Slovenian and other Slavic cuisines. The cabbage and meat can be layered in a baking dish, almost like a casserole. More commonly, the meat mixture is rolled into a large piece of cabbage, tied, and then cooked as a cabbage roll. Sauces can be made of meat gravy, tomatoes, or even sauerkraut. Cabbage rolls are generally made with green cabbage but, for an unusual flavor, red cabbage may also be used. The following recipe includes rice; if you leave out the rice, serve the sarma with boiled potatoes.

Serves 6 to 8

1 large head cabbage
2 or 3 slices bacon, cut into small pieces
1 medium onion, peeled and chopped
1 pound ground beef or pork
1 teaspoon salt
Freshly ground pepper
1 egg
1½ cups rice, cooked (optional)
2 cloves garlic, peeled and crushed
2 to 3 tablespoons lard, oil or butter
1 bay leaf
2 cups stewed tomatoes, or 2 pounds fresh
1 cup sour cream

1. Remove the dirty leaves of the cabbage from the cabbage head. Place the head of cabbage in a pot of boiling water for just 3 to 4 minutes. Remove the cabbage once the leaves are tender but still firm, and are easy to remove in whole pieces.

2. Remove the cabbage from the pot. Allow to cool. Remove the leaves from the head of cabbage, one by one, and set aside.

3. In a large skillet, cook the bacon and onion over medium heat for 5 to 8 minutes, or until the bacon is browned. Add the meat, salt and pepper. Cook until the meat is cooked through, 5 to 8 minutes.

4. Remove from heat and allow to cool. Mix in the egg, rice and garlic.

5. To make the cabbage rolls, place a few spoonfuls of the meat mixture on each cabbage leaf. Roll up the cabbage leaf and either tie with a string, or fasten with a toothpick.

6. In a large saucepan, heat the lard or oil over medium heat. Place the cabbage rolls, 2 or 3 at a time, in the pan, and cook for 4 to 6 minutes on each side, or until browned. Once all the cabbage rolls are browned, place all of the cabbage rolls back into the pan.

Fill the pan ¾ full with water and add the bay leaf.

7. Partially cover the pan with a lid. Allow the rolls to cook slowly over medium heat for 30 to 40 minutes, or until the cabbage is tender.

8. Remove the rolls from the pan and keep warm. Add the tomatoes to the pan and continue to cook for 8 to 10 minutes, stirring occasionally, until a thickened sauce has formed. Remove the bay leaf.

9. Remove the pan from the heat. Stir in the sour cream. Season the sauce with salt and pepper, to taste.

10. Serve the cabbage rolls with the sauce and potatoes, if you wish.

Roasted Trout *Pečena Postrv*

Trout is found in many of the mountain streams around Slovenia, especially in the northwestern mountainous region. Roast trout is often served with a parsley, olive oil, and garlic sauce, the recipe for which is included here. Fish are usually served whole. Although removing the head and bones as one eats may sound like a lot of extra work, receiving a whole fish ensures that one has received a local, fresh trout. You may notice locals looking into the eyes of the fish before eating it to make sure it is very fresh.

Serves 4

Fish:
2 pound trout
Juice of 1 lemon
½ teaspoon salt
Freshly ground pepper
3 slices white bread,
  crumbled or cubed
2 to 3 tablespoons olive oil

Sauce:
2 cups (or 1 bunch) parsley,
  cleaned and chopped
1 cup good-quality olive
  oil
Juice of 1 lemon
4 cloves garlic, peeled and
  minced
Salt and freshly ground
  pepper

1. Prepare the fish: clean it, inside and out. Sprinkle with lemon juice, salt and pepper.
2. Roll the fish in the bread crumbs.
3. Heat the olive oil in a skillet over medium heat.
4. Add the trout to the pan. Cook over medium to high heat for 5 to 6 minutes on each side.
5. When the fish is slightly browned on each side, and the meat is cooked through, the trout is done.
6. To make the sauce, combine the parsley, olive oil, lemon juice, garlic, salt and pepper.
7. Serve the trout with the sauce and boiled potatoes. A light white wine, such as a Malvazija, served cold, will go well with this meal.

Dormouse Stew Polhara Obara

The dormouse is a nocturnal, tree-dwelling rodent. Because this European cousin to the squirrel is edible, the dormouse is popular fare in the Notranjska region of Slovenia, and a lot of tradition surrounds the hunting and eating of it. One can visit the Dormouse Museum in Cerknica, and Dormouse Night (Polharska Noč), is celebrated in October during the dormouse-hunting season. According to Slovenian legend, the dormouse is actually possessed by the devil himself, and fully deserves to be hunted down and thrown into the stewpot. The marjoram and parsley in this recipe add a nice flavor. Chicken is a tasty substitute for the dormouse, and far less gamy.

Serves 4

4 dormice (you may
   substitute 1 whole
   chicken), boneless,
   unskinned
4 tablespoons (½ stick)
   butter or oil
½ cup all-purpose flour
1 pound potatoes, peeled
   and cubed
1 teaspoon salt
2 tablespoons chopped
   fresh parsley
2 tablespoons fresh
   marjoram or 2 teaspoons
   dried
2 or 3 peppercorns
Grated peel of 1 lemon
1 tablespoon vinegar

1. Cut the meat into medium-size pieces. In a large skillet, heat the butter or oil. Fry the meat over medium to high heat for 10 to 12 minutes, or until the meat is browned.
2. Add the flour, and stir. Continue to cook over medium heat for another 3 to 4 minutes.
3. Add enough water to the pan to cover the meat.
4. Add the potatoes, salt, parsley, marjoram, peppercorns and lemon peel. Cover and cook over medium heat for about 30 minutes.
5. When the potatoes and meat are tender, the stew is ready. If the sauce is watery, cook uncovered until some of the water has evaporated, and the sauce is thick.
6. Add the vinegar and stir. Serve hot.

Carniolan Sausages Kranjske Klobase

Homemade sausages remain a big part of Slovenian cuisine. Made during the slaughter, sausages include a variety of animal parts and seasonings. They are a great way to use up the bits and pieces of the animal that are difficult to eat in any other way. A lot of salt is used, which helps to preserve the meat. In the days before refrigeration, the fresh sausages were smoked and then stored completely covered in lard, to be preserved from exposure to the air. Nowadays, sausages can be smoked or steamed, and later roasted or even sliced and served cold. The following recipe presents the most popular smoked sausage in Slovenia, and comes from the mountainous Gorenska region in the northwest.

Makes 5 pounds

¼ pound sausage casing,
   or pig intestine
1 head garlic
1 cup water
5 pounds pork, some lean
   and some fat, coarsely
   ground
¼ cup salt
1½ tablespoons pepper
1 tablespoon paprika
   (optional)

1. Soak the casings for several hours in luke-warm water. Run water through them to make sure they are clean.

2. Peel the garlic cloves and crush them. Place them in a clean cloth, and tie the cloth, forming a "garlic bag." Place this cloth and its contents into 1 cup of water. Let this stand for several hours. Remove the cloth and garlic, and keep the garlic-infused water.

3. In a very large bowl, combine the pork, salt, pepper, garlic water, and paprika, if you wish. Mix it well.

4. Let the meat mixture rest for 30 minutes, and mix it again. Cover and let stand for several hours, or refrigerate overnight.

5. Tie a knot at one end of the casing. Either with a funnel, or a stuffing nozzle, stuff the meat mixture into the casing. Twist the casing every 5 or 6 inches, to form the sausages. Tie off the end of the casing.

6. Prick a small hole in each sausage to make sure that no air is caught in the sausages.

7. Let the sausages rest in the refrigerator for 1 day.

8. The sausages then need to be smoked for 4 to 5 days. If you do not have a smoker, you may ask your local butcher to smoke them for you. Or you may roast them in a barbecue pit. If you are smoking them yourself, use a hard wood such as hickory or oak. Make sure that you are using smoke and not flames. Turn the sausages every few hours while they are smoking.

9. Let the sausages cool for a day or so in a cool, protected place.

10. You may store them in the refrigerator or the freezer.

11. When you are ready to serve them, you may fry or roast them, or simply slice them.

Traditional Spicy Meatballs Čevapčiči

Čevapčiči is a grilled, spiced meatball with its roots in the southern Balkans. Often sold on the street as a quick snack or lunch, čevapčiči is served on the streets of Ljubljana. Resembling a rolled, spicy hamburger, čevapčiči is typically served with fresh bread, onions, peppers, ajvar *(see recipe for ajvar on page 211), and a cold beer. It is also traditionally recommended that čevapčiči be served with a good prayer.*

Serves 4 to 6

2 pounds finely ground
  lamb or pork, or a
  combination of the two
1 tablespoon sweet paprika
1 large onion, peeled and
  finely chopped
1 egg, slightly beaten
2 cloves garlic, peeled and
  minced
2 teaspoons salt
Freshly ground pepper
2 to 3 tablespoons olive oil

1. Combine all of the ingredients except for the oil. The mixture should be sticky.
2. Form the meat mixture into small rolls, approximately 3 inches long and ½ to 1 inch in diameter.
3. Place the čevapčiči on a dish or tray, and brush with the oil.
4. Grill the čevapčiči on an outdoor or indoor grill on high heat. Flip them as you would a hamburger. Continue to cook for 5 to 6 minutes per side until they are evenly browned on the outside and well done on the inside. (You may also broil them, if you do not have a grill.)
5. Serve the čevapčiči with ajvar (see the recipe on page 211), chopped onions, fresh tomatoes, sliced peppers, and fresh, crusty bread.

Blood Sausages (Black Pudding)

Krvave Klobase

The blood that is saved during the pig slaughter adds not only a strong flavor and color to these sausages, but also a lot of protein.

Makes 6 to 8 pounds

1 pig's head (traditionally,
  pig's tongue, snouts,
  cheeks, or jowls are used),
  or 5 pounds pork meat
1 pig's liver, cooked
1 pig's lung, cooked
8 cups pig's blood
1 pound lard or cracklings,
  melted
1 tablespoon salt
1 teaspoon freshly ground
  pepper
1 teaspoon dried marjoram
1 tablespoon ground
  cinnamon
1 teaspoon ground cloves
1 pound sausage casings or
  pig intestine

1. If you are collecting the pig's blood during slaughter, make sure to stir it continuously while it cools, to make sure that it does not congeal.

2. Cook the pig's tongue, snouts, cheeks or jowls in boiling water for 25 to 35 minutes, or until tender. Remove the meat, and save the stock.

3. Coarsely grind or chop all the meat, except for the tongue. Cut the tongue into 1 or 2 inch pieces.

4. Combine the meat with the blood, lard, salt, pepper, marjoram, cinnamon and cloves.

5. Soak the casings in lukewarm water, and make sure they are clean.

6. Tie a knot at one end of the casing. Either with a funnel, or a stuffing nozzle, stuff the meat mixture into the casing. Cut the casing every 8 or 10 inches, to form the sausages. Tie off each end of the casing, making sure there are no air bubbles in the sausage. Prick a small hole in each sausage to make sure that no air is caught in the sausages.

7. Cook the sausages in the stock that you have saved from boiling the meat, or in boiling water for 25 to 30 minutes.

8. Remove the sausages from the boiling water, and let cool for 1 to 2 days, refrigerated.

9. You may store them in the refrigerator or freezer. To eat, you may slice them and eat them cold, or fry them or roast them in the oven.

THE LEGEND OF ZLATOROG, THE GOLDEN-HORNED CHAMOIS

In the mid 1800s, during a period of Romantic nationalism for Slovenians, a legend developed around the formation of the Triglav Lakes Valley. Zlatorog, a mythical chamois with golden horns, lived on Mount Triglav and guarded its treasure. He roamed the valley, at that time a large, beautiful garden, with good fairies known as the White Ladies. The White Ladies kept the pastures of the valley green, and granted good deeds to humans in need.

Meanwhile, down in the Soča Valley, a greedy innkeeper's wife became jealous when her daughter was given jewels by a wealthy Venetian merchant. The mother insisted that the girl's lover, a local hunter of modest means, match this wealth to gain her hand in marriage. She demanded that he bring back Zlatorog's gold, hidden under Mount Bogatin and guarded by a multi-headed serpent. At the very least, he was told, he must bring back a bunch of Triglav roses, impossible to find in the winter months, to prove his love.

The hunter, mad with jealousy, headed into the mountains in search of Zlatorog. He found the chamois, and shot him with a direct hit. The blood from Zlatorog's wound melted the surrounding snow, and up sprung a bunch of Triglav roses. Zlatorog ate a few of the rose petals and was immediately restored. The chamois turned to climb into the mountains, leaving more Triglav roses in his trail, enticing the hunter to follow him. As they climbed higher and higher, the hunter was distracted by sunlight reflecting off of Zlatorog's golden horns. He lost his footing, and fell into a gorge.

The trusting Zlatorog was so angry that a human would betray him that he gouged the valley with his horns, creating the lakes and valleys that are there today. He and the White Ladies left the valley, never to return. In the spring, when the snow melted, the lifeless body of the hunter was delivered to the valley in the rushing waters of the Soča River. When the girl found the body of her lover, his cold hand was still clutching a Triglav rose.

The Slovenian national seal, also featured on the Slovenian flag, prominently displays the three peaks of Mount Triglav.

MOUNT TRIGLAV

Reaching 2,864 meters (9,394 feet), Mount Triglav in the Bohinj Valley is the highest peak in all of the former Yugoslavia.

Triglav, literally meaning "three heads," was thought by early Slavs to be ruled by a three-headed deity. This deity ruled the sky, the earth, and the underworld. No one dared climb the peak until the late eighteenth century. The summit was first reached by an Austrian mountaineer who climbed Triglav from Lake Bohinj, with his three Slovenian guides in 1778. Under Habsburg rule in the nineteenth century, during the wave of Slovenian nationalism, the pilgrimage to Triglav became an important event for Slovenians wanting to confirm their Slovenian identity.

Although this hike can be difficult and will take at least two days, this tradition continues today. A true Slovenian is expected to climb Mount Triglav at least once in his or her life.

THE LEGEND OF MARTIN KRPAN

Another Slavic legend that gained popularity during the Slovenian nationalist revival in the mid-1800s was the story of the gentle giant, Martin Krpan. Slavic folklore tells of many larger-than-life heroes who uproot trees with their hands, have loud voices and carry large weapons, and wear shoes five times larger than the average human. Martin Krpan is the most popular of these characters.

Krpan, it is believed, came from the Notranjska region of Slovenia, in the north. He had a heart of gold, but was wanted by the law for smuggling salt. When he was arrested by royal guards, he demonstrated his tremendous strength to the emperor of Vienna by picking up and carrying his horse. The emperor was impressed.

The emperor decided to use Krpan's strength for fighting the local troublemaker, Berdavs, described as a marauding Turk. Krpan successfully defeated Berdavs by chopping off his head with his magic ax. The emperor rewarded Krpan with free transportation and a monopoly on the trade of salt.

This legend was published by the author Fran Levstik in 1858. In doing so, he raised the status of the local legend of Martin Krpan, and the local Slovenian language. With his work, Levstik popularized a hero that all Slovenes could admire.

Cakes, Breads, and Strudels

Ne stori kruha moka, temveč roka.
It is not the flour that makes the bread,
  but the baker.

— Slovenian proverb

Kdor košček kruha zametuje
  drobtinic večkrat mu zmanjkuje!
He who doesn't value every piece of bread is
  often short of crumbs.

— Slovenian proverb

Walnut Potica Orehova Potica

Potica, a rolled yeast bread filled with a variety of fillings, is very much a Slovenian dish. The word potica is derived from the Slovenian word poviti *meaning "to wrap in." Slovenian women pride themselves on their potica, which is served at many family gatherings and festive occasions. Every household has its favorite recipe. One collection of traditional Slovenian recipes includes seven versions of walnut potica, for example. The sweet versions can be served with coffee or as a dessert with a glass of dry white wine. A slice of a savory potica can be served with the main meal, or as a snack with a cold glass of beer. The most popular version of potica is filled with walnuts and raisins, but fillings can include dried pears, honey, chocolate, pumpkin seeds, tarragon, or pork cracklings. Use your favorite ingredients to create your own fillings!*

Serves 12

Yeast Starter:
1 cake (2 ounce) fresh compressed yeast or 3 packages (¼ ounce each) dry yeast
1 tablespoon sugar
½ cup milk, warmed slightly

Dough:
5 egg yolks, slightly beaten (save the whites for the filling)
¾ cup butter (1½ sticks), melted
1½ cups whole milk or cream, warmed slightly
1 tablespoon vanilla extract
2 tablespoons rum
7 cups all-purpose flour, sifted
2 teaspoons salt

1. Place the yeast, 1 tablespoon sugar, and ½ cup of warm milk in a small bowl or cup. Cover, and let stand in a warm, protected place for 20 to 30 minutes, or until it becomes foamy and rises.

2. In a medium bowl, combine the wet ingredients for the dough: egg yolks, melted butter, whole milk, vanilla, and rum.

3. In a large bowl, combine 6½ cups of the flour with the dry ingredients for the dough: salt, sugar, and lemon rind. Form a well in the center.

4. Add the egg yolk mixture to the flour and begin to stir.

5. Slowly add the yeast mixture to the dough.

6. With a wooden spoon, mix until all liquid has been absorbed into the dough.

7. Turn the dough out onto a well-floured surface. Knead for 10 minutes, or until you see bubbles appear in the dough. Add the remaining flour as needed if the dough is sticky.

8. Place the dough in a greased bowl, cover, and let sit in a warm, protected place to let it

½ cup sugar
1 tablespoon grated lemon
rind

Walnut Filling:
2 pounds walnuts, ground
finely
½ cup butter (1 stick),
melted
1½ cups whole milk or
cream, warmed
1 cup sugar
¾ cup honey
1 tablespoon vanilla
extract
Grated peel from 1 lemon
1 teaspoon ground
cinnamon
5 egg whites, beaten until
stiff
1 to 2 cups raisins
(optional)

Topping:
1 egg, slightly beaten,
or 3 tablespoons milk or
cream

rise for about 1 hour, or until the dough has doubled in size.

9. In the meantime, prepare the walnut filling. Combine the walnuts, butter, milk, sugar, honey, vanilla, lemon and cinnamon. Once these ingredients have been combined, gently fold in the egg whites. Add the raisins, if you desire.

10. Let the walnut mixture stand until it is cooled. It should not be too thick, but easily spreadable, like a thick frosting. You may add more warm milk to obtain the right consistency.

11. Once the dough has doubled in size, roll it out onto a well-floured surface with a rolling pin. Sprinkle only enough additional flour on the dough so as to avoid the rolling pin sticking to the dough. Roll into a rectangular shape to a thickness of approximately ¾ inch.

12. Spread the walnut filling on the entire surface of the dough, leaving 1 inch at one edge of the dough, which will become the end of the roll.

13. Roll the dough tightly, beginning at the edge opposite the edge with the clean one inch of dough. Roll as tightly as you can. Beginning halfway through the rolling, prick the dough here and there with a fork, so as to prevent the potica from cracking while baking.

14. Continue to roll until 1 inch from the end. Brush this area with slightly beaten egg, to create a seal, and complete the roll.

15. Place the rolled potica into a well-greased baking dish. You may wind it into a round cake tin, or cut it in half and lay the pieces straight in a rectangular baking dish.

(continued)

16. Cover the potica with a cloth and let sit in a warm, well-protected place, allowing the dough to rise once again. Let it sit for 30 to 60 minutes, or until it has doubled in size.

17. Before putting the potica in the oven, brush the top with the beaten egg or a few tablespoons of milk.

18. Preheat the oven to 325°F. Bake the potica in the preheated oven for approximately 1 hour and 15 minutes. Keep an eye on the potica. It should be golden brown on the top, and the dough should be cooked thoroughly. If the top becomes too brown and the dough is not yet done, you may cover it with aluminum foil until the dough is cooked through.

19. Remove the potica from the oven. Let cool completely before cutting into it.

20. You may coat the top with sugar or icing, if you wish. This potica goes particularly well with a strong cup of coffee or hot tea.

Pumkpin Seed Potica Potica iz Bučnih Semen

This is a great recipe for the fall!

Serves 12

Yeast Starter and Dough:
Use the same ingredients and steps as outlined in the recipe for Walnut Potica, pages 156–158, eliminating the rum and lemon peel.

Filling:
2 tablespoons butter
2 cups pumpkin seeds, husked and chopped
¾ cup sugar
1 teaspoon vanilla extract
¼ pound (1 stick) butter, melted
2 egg yolks, slightly beaten
2 egg whites, beaten until stiff

1. Prepare the yeast and dough for the potica as in the recipe for Walnut Potica, pages 156–158.

2. In the meantime, make the pumpkin seed filling: In a saucepan, melt the 2 tablespoons butter. Add the pumpkin seeds, ¼ cup of the sugar and the vanilla, stirring continuously. Once the seeds are browned, remove the pan from heat and let cool.

3. In a large bowl, combine the melted butter, egg yolks, and remaining ½ cup sugar. Fold in the stiff egg whites. Add the pumpkin seeds.

4. Roll out the dough as described in the recipe for Walnut Potica, and spread the pumpkin seed filling on the dough.

5. Continue to prepare and bake the potica as in the recipe for Walnut Potica.

Raisin Potica *Rozinova Potica*

For this recipe, be sure to soak the raisins well in advance of preparing the dough. The longer they soak, the more flavorful they will be.

Serves 12

Yeast Starter and Dough:
Use the same ingredients and steps as outlined in the recipe for Walnut Potica, pages 156–158, with two exceptions: instead of the lemon peel and rum, add 1 cup of sour cream to the wet ingredients for the dough.

Filling:
2 boxes (15 ounces each) golden raisins
½ to 1 cup wine or liqueur
¼ pound (1 stick) butter, melted
¼ cup brown sugar
1 cup sugar
1 cup sour cream
6 egg yolks, slightly beaten
2 tablespoons grated lemon peel
2 cups bread crumbs, made with white bread
6 egg whites, beaten stiff

Topping:
1 egg, beaten slightly or 3 tablespoons milk or cream

1. Allow the raisins to soak in the wine or liqueur for 1 to 2 days before making the potica. Stir occasionally.
2. Prepare the yeast and dough, following the recipe for Walnut Potica on pages 156–158, through step #8.
3. To prepare the raisin filling, combine the butter, brown and white sugars, sour cream, egg yolks, lemon peel and bread crumbs. Gently fold in the stiff egg whites. Once the ingredients are combined, set the filling aside to cool.
4. Once the dough has doubled in size, roll it out onto a well-floured surface with a rolling pin. Sprinkle only enough additional flour on the dough so as to avoid the rolling pin from sticking to the dough. Roll out to a rectangular shape to a thickness of approximately ¾ inch.
5. Spread the filling on the entire surface of the dough, leaving one inch at one edge of the dough, which will become the end of the roll.
6. Drain the raisins. Sprinkle the raisins on top of the filling so as to cover the entire surface evenly.
7. Roll the dough tightly, beginning at the edge opposite the edge with the clean one inch of dough. Roll as tightly as you can. Beginning halfway through the rolling, prick the dough here and there with a fork, so as to prevent the potica from cracking while baking.

8. Continue to roll until 1 inch from the end. Brush this area with slightly beaten egg, as to create a seal, and complete the roll.

9. Place the rolled potica into a well-greased baking dish. You may wind it into a round cake tin, or cut it in half and lay the pieces straight in a rectangular baking dish.

10. Cover the potica with a cloth and let sit in a warm, well-protected place, allowing the dough to rise once again. Let it sit for 30 to 60 minutes, or until it has doubled in size.

11. Before putting the potica in the oven, brush the top with the beaten egg or a few tablespoons of milk.

12. Bake in an oven which has been pre-heated to 325°F for approximately 45 minutes to 1 hour, or until golden brown on the top, and the dough is cooked thoroughly.

13. Remove the potica from the oven. Let cool completely before cutting into it.

Tarragon Potica _Pehtranova Potica_

This is an example of a savory potica.

Serves 12

Yeast Starter:
1 cake (2 ounce) fresh
  compressed yeast or 3
  packages (¼ ounce each)
  dry yeast
¼ cup milk, warmed
  slightly
1 tablespoon sugar
3 tablespoons all-purpose
  flour

Dough:
1½ cups milk
2 tablespoons butter
1 egg
1 egg yolk, slightly beaten
1 tablespoon sugar
1 teaspoon salt
4 cups all-purpose flour,
  sifted

Filling:
5 tablespoons butter
⅓ cup fresh bread crumbs
3 egg yolks, beaten slightly
2 tablespoons sugar
1 cup sour cream
2 tablespoons chopped
  fresh tarragon, or 2
  teaspoons dried tarragon
1 egg white, beaten stiff

1. Dissolve the yeast in the ¼ cup of luke-warm milk. Add 1 tablespoon sugar and 3 tablespoons flour. Cover, and let stand in a warm, protected place for 20 to 30 minutes, or until it becomes foamy and rises.
2. For the dough, heat the 1½ cups of milk in a saucepan. Add the butter and keep over low to medium heat until the butter melts. Pour milk and butter into a large bowl. Allow to cool.
3. Once the milk and butter mixture has cooled, add the 1 whole egg, 1 egg yolk, sugar and salt. Beat well.
4. Add the sifted flour to the egg yolk mixture.
5. Add the yeast mixture to the dough.
6. With a wooden spoon, combine all the ingredients until you have a smooth dough.
7. Turn the dough out onto a well-floured surface. Knead for 10 minutes, or until you see bubbles appear in the dough. Add additional flour as needed if the dough is sticky.
8. Place the dough in a greased bowl, cover, and let sit in a warm, protected place to let it rise for about 1 hour, or until the dough has doubled in size.
9. In the meantime, prepare the tarragon filling. Melt the 5 tablespoons of butter in a saucepan, add the bread crumbs, and cook stirring continuously, until the bread crumbs are browned.
10. In a bowl, combine the egg yolks, sugar, sour cream and tarragon. Slowly add the bread crumbs, stirring continuously. Fold in the beaten egg white.

For the top of the dough:
1 egg, slightly beaten,
 or 3 tablespoons milk or
 cream

11. Grease an angel food or bundt cake pan well.

12. Once the dough has doubled in size, roll it out onto a well-floured surface with a rolling pin. Sprinkle only enough additional flour on the dough to avoid the rolling pin from sticking to the dough. Roll out a rectangular shape to a thickness of approximately ¼ inch.

13. Spread the tarragon filling on the entire surface of the dough, leaving 1 inch at one edge of the dough, which will become the end of the roll.

14. Roll the dough tightly, beginning at the edge opposite the edge with the clean 1 inch of dough. Roll as tightly as you can.

15. Place the rolled potica into the greased round baking pan.

16. Cover the potica with a cloth and let sit in a warm, well-protected place, allowing the dough to rise once again. Let it sit for 30 to 60 minutes, or until it has doubled in size.

17. Before putting the potica in the oven, brush the tops with the beaten egg or a few tablespoons of milk or cream.

18. Bake in an oven which has been preheated to 325°F for approximately 1 hour. Keep an eye on the potica. It should be golden brown on the top, and the dough should be cooked thoroughly.

19. Remove the potica from the oven. Let it stand for at least 15 minutes before you remove it from the pan.

20. Serve with lunch or with a glass of beer as a snack!

Angel Wings Krhki Flancati

Flancati are light, flaky pastries sprinkled with confectioners sugar, which are often served at special occasions. At weddings, for example, baskets of them are available for nibbling, as a dessert or to accompany a glass of wine. They can be stored in a tightly sealed container to maintain their freshness. Many households have them on hand for unexpected guests.

Makes approximately 50 cookies

4 egg yolks
½ cup sour cream
½ teaspoon salt
½ cup granulated sugar
2 tablespoons lemon juice
2 tablespoons rum or brandy
2½ to 3 cups all-purpose flour
Vegetable oil, shortening, or lard, for frying
Confectioners' sugar to coat the pastries

1. In a large bowl, combine the egg yolks, sour cream, salt, sugar, lemon juice, and rum. Slowly add the flour, stirring continuously, until you have formed a soft, manageable dough.

2. Turn the dough out onto a floured surface. Knead for approximately 10 minutes.

3. Divide the dough into 3 large balls. Place the dough on a floured surface and cover with a cloth. Let it rest for about 30 to 60 minutes.

4. Taking 1 ball of dough at a time, roll the dough out onto a floured surface until the dough is approximately ¼ inch thick.

5. Cut 2½-inch x 3-inch rectangles out of the dough with either a sharp knife or a crimped edge cutter.

6. You may create interesting shapes with the dough before frying. For example, make one or two parallel incisions in the center of the rectangle. Pull one of the opposite corners of the dough through the incision, forming a twist or a "butterfly" shape.

7. In a large skillet, heat the oil for frying over medium heat. Once you have shaped the dough, drop it immediately into the hot fat. Drop 3 or 4 in at a time. Fry quickly until they are golden brown, about 30 seconds on each side. You do not want them to get too dark, nor do you want them to sit in the fat for too long. Adjust the heat of the fat as necessary.

8. When they are done cooking, place the pastries on a paper towel to drain.

9. Sprinkle them with confectioners' sugar while still hot.

Honey Biscuits Škofjeloški Medeni Kruhki

These spicy cookies, almost like gingerbread, come from the Gorenjska region of Slovenia. The history of beekeeping is important to this region, as are honey and honey-based products. These cookies can be hard, and are often made in molds with elaborate carvings to create decorated cookies for the holidays. They can also be decorated with colored frosting. But not just for decoration, these cookies are delicious!

Makes 60 cookies

4 cups all-purpose flour
3 tablespoons baking
  powder
1½ cups honey
1 tablespoon ground
  cinnamon
¼ teaspoon ground cloves
¼ teaspoon grated nutmeg
Grated lemon peel and
  juice from 1 lemon
4 tablespoons oil or butter,
  melted
¼ cup rum or whiskey

1. Sift together the flour and baking powder into a large bowl.
2. Warm the honey until liquid. Add the honey, spices, lemon rind and juice, oil and whiskey to the flour mixture. Stir with a wooden spoon until a dough is formed.
3. Roll the dough out to a floured surface, and knead well.
4. Return the dough to the bowl. Cover and let rest at room temperature for 2 days.
5. On the third day, place the dough in a baking tin and let it sit in a warm oven (100°F or so) for 45 minutes or until the dough is softened.
6. On a floured surface, roll the dough out until it is ¼ inch thick.
7. Using a heart-shaped (or other style) cookie cutter, cut the dough and place the cookies on a well-greased cookie sheet.
8. Bake at 300°F for 10 minutes. Remove the cookies from the oven and brush them with honey heated with a little water. Return to the oven for another 5 minutes.
9. Decorate with frosting as you wish.
10. Store in a tightly closed container. They are hard, but will soften a little if they are stored in a humid place.

HONEY AND BEEKEEPING IN SLOVENIA

Čebela je kot beseda; ima med in želo.
A bee is like a word; it has honey and a sting.

– Slovenian proverb

Man has depended on honey as a food and a medicine for thousands of years. However, not until the nineteenth century did modern beekeeping develop as we know it today in Slovenia. Bees naturally use hollow trees or underground holes to build their hives. Hundreds of years ago, man would use hollow logs cut to size and filled with straw to create beehives. This method became widespread in fifteenth-century Europe. However, the "hives" would have to be destroyed to harvest the honey at the end of every season.

The first mention of beehives made of boards is in "The Glory of the Duchy of Carniola," written by the Slovenian scientist Janez Vajkard Valvasor in 1689. In the mid-eighteenth century, honeycomb boxes were invented in Kranjić, allowing the combs to be moved like drawers. This was an important turning point in apiculture. Anton Janša, a well-known Slovenian teacher of apiculture, developed the method of smoking bees out of their hive to collect the honey. Born in Gorenjska in 1734, he is known as the father of modern beekeeping. He also developed ways of transporting bees and dispatching them to other fields, and founded the

Carniolan Grey bee species, an important contribution to the industry. He also wrote two well-known books on apiculture. An apicultural school was set up in Slovenia in the late eighteenth century, modeling itself after its Viennese equivalent.

Beekeeping in Slovenia has contributed the country's most popular form of folk art with the creation of painted beehive doors, *panjske končnice*. Dating as far back as the mid-eighteenth century, these painted wooden panels were made at monasteries and originally depicted religious scenes, such as the 1758 Mary Holding Jesus beehive door. Between 1820 and 1880, panjske končnice became all the rage and the scenes became profane, depicting humorous or satirical scenes from Slovenian folklore. As examples, a traditional beehive door depicts the devil sharpening a woman's tongue, or two farmers fighting over a cow while the lawyer milks the cow. There are also scenes of a "world turned upside down" in which the animals carry guns and carry the hunter off to his grave. The panels were painted by professional artists and amateurs alike, using paint prepared with linseed oil, ensuring their longevity. This form of art ended in the early nineteenth century, when larger hives were built. The traditional-style panels are still made today for sale as souvenirs and gifts.

Bees and honey are still important in today's Slovenia. Honey is produced and sold all over the country for use in bread, cakes and cookies. Beeswax is used to make decorative candles. Mead (*medeno žganje*) is a honey brandy, which is considered to have medicinal purposes. Pollen, propolis, and royal jelly are all used in homeopathic medicine.

Harvesting honey in the Slovenian countryside, postcard by
Maksim Gaspari.

Shrovetide Doughnuts Vzhajani Krofi

In Slovenia, it is traditional to bake and serve doughnuts on Shrove Tuesday (Fat Tuesday), the day preceding Ash Wednesday and the beginning of Lent on the Christian calendar. These homemade doughnuts are light and airy, and are often filled with jam or fruit preserves. They are served with coffee in the morning or afternoon, or with a glass of wine in the early evening.

Makes 36 doughnuts

Yeast Starter:
1 cake (2 ounce) fresh
  compressed yeast or 3
  packages (¼ ounce each)
  dry yeast
2 tablespoons sugar
½ cup milk, slightly
  warmed

Dough:
1½ cups milk or cream
¼ pound butter (1 stick)
3 eggs
½ cup sugar
1 teaspoon salt
1 cup sour cream
Grated rind and juice of 1
  lemon
¼ cup rum
6 to 7 cups all-purpose
  flour

Apricot jam for filling
  (optional)
Vegetable oil, shortening,
  or lard, for frying
Confectioners' sugar,
  for sprinkling

1. Combine the yeast, 2 tablespoons sugar, and ½ cup of warm milk in a small bowl or cup. Cover and let stand in a warm, protected place for 20 to 30 minutes, or until it becomes foamy and rises.

2. In a large saucepan, heat the 1½ cups milk or cream and butter until the butter has melted. Remove from heat and allow to cool.

3. In a large bowl, beat the eggs and add sugar, salt and sour cream. Stir until combined. Add the milk and butter mixture.

4. Add the yeast, lemon rind and juice, rum and 2 cups of flour. Stir until smooth.

5. Gradually mix in up to 5 cups of flour. Continue to add enough flour to keep the dough manageable.

6. Turn the dough out on a floured surface and knead about 10 minutes, until you have formed a soft, non-sticking dough. You may add more flour to the kneading surface, if necessary.

7. Place the dough in a greased bowl. Cover and let stand in a warm, well-protected area. Allow the dough to rise for 1½ to 2 hours, or until it has doubled in size.

8. Roll the dough out onto a floured surface, and stretch the dough (do not roll it) to a thickness of ½ inch.

9. With a glass or round cookie cutter, cut out rounds of dough to make the doughnuts. You may also cut a hole in the center, if so desired (for an "American style" doughnut).

10. If you would like jam filled doughnuts, place a ½ teaspoon of jam or preserves in the center of one round of dough. Take a second round of dough and place on top of the first. Seal the edges well, so that the jam does not leak while frying.

11. Place the dough rounds on a clean surface and cover with a cloth. Allow them to rise for 30 minutes, or until they are light and fluffy.

12. In a large skillet, heat the oil for frying over medium heat. You do not want the fat to be too hot.

13. Test the temperature of the oil for frying. Fry one of the doughnuts in the oil for 4 to 6 minutes. It should turn a light golden brown on one side while floating in the oil. Then flip it to the other side until the second side is also golden brown. The doughnut should not cook too quickly or become dark brown, but slowly enough so that the dough is cooked all the way through. Adjust the heat as necessary. You may test the doughnut with a toothpick.

14. Continue to fry the remaining doughnuts. When done, let them drain on a paper towel. Sprinkle with confectioners' sugar while they are still hot.

Christmas Bread or Braided Sweet Bread Božičnik or Praznični Kruh

Bread plays a central role in Christmas traditions in Slovenia. Representing prosperity and sustenance, special loaves of bread are baked for the holiday season. In Bela Krajina, the southeastern corner of Slovenia, Christmas bread is a large round loaf that is decorated with the figures of the nativity scene, also made of bread. This specially decorated loaf is placed in the center of the kitchen table on Christmas Eve, and remains there until it is eaten on New Year's Day. Traditionally, the mother of the household places her best white tablecloth on the table, sprinkling seeds and dried herbs underneath to represent a good harvest for the following year. She then puts the Christmas bread, Božičnik, on the cloth. The kitchen table is not used for any other reason during this time, as it is the focal point of the kitchen and represents God's goodness and generosity to the family. The same dough for Christmas bread is also used to make braided bread, another holiday treat.

Makes 2 loaves

Yeast Starter:
2 packages (¼ ounce each) dry yeast
2 tablespoons sugar
¼ cup warm water

Dough:
3 cups milk
¼ pound butter (1 stick), softened
½ cup sugar
1 teaspoon salt
3 eggs, slightly beaten
5 to 6 cups all-purpose flour

1. Mix the yeast, 2 tablespoons sugar and ¼ cup warm water in a cup or small bowl. Cover and let stand in a warm, protected place for 20 to 30 minutes, or until it bubbles and the yeast rises.

2. In a large saucepan, heat the milk (do not let it boil) with the butter until the butter melts. Remove from heat and let cool.

3. In a large bowl, mix the ½ cup sugar, salt and 3 eggs with the cooled milk mixture. Add the yeast. Mix in 3 cups of flour. Stir until smooth.

4. Continue adding flour until you have created a soft dough that is easy to work with.

5. Cover and place in a warm, protected place. Let rise until it has doubled in size (1 to 2 hours).

6. Divide the dough into 6 equal parts. Form a 12-inch long roll with each piece of dough.

Topping:
1 egg, beaten
Almonds, for garnish
  (optional)

7. Take 3 pieces of the dough and braid them together. Pinch the ends. Do the same with the remaining 3 pieces of dough.

8. Place each loaf in a well-greased loaf pan, or on a cookie sheet. Cover, and place in a warm protected place. Let the dough rise again until the loaves have doubled in size (about 1 hour).

9. Brush the top of each loaf with the beaten egg. Sprinkle with sliced or slivered almonds, if you wish.

10. Bake at 350°F for 45 to 50 minutes, or until the loaves are slightly browned and baked all the way through.

VEŚELE BOŽIČNE PRAZNIKE!

A humorous Christmas card from Maksim Gaspari.

Easter Bread Velikonočni Kruhki

*Easter is an important holiday in Slovenia, not only because of its signifi-
cance in the Christian faith, but also because it symbolizes the rebirth of the
Earth at springtime. Good Friday is a day of great sadness and fasting. Holy
Saturday is the first redemptive day after Lent; fire is blessed early in the
morning, Christ's Mass of Resurrection is celebrated, eggs are colored, and in
the afternoon there is a blessing of Easter food called* žegen. *Easter Sunday is
a day of great celebration and festivities, beginning on Sunday morning with
the eating of the* žegen, *which centers around this* Velikonočni kruhki.

Makes 10 to 12 small loaves

1 package (½ ounce)
  dry yeast
⅓ cup warm milk
2 tablespoons sugar
2½ to 3 cups all-purpose
  flour
½ teaspoon ground
  cardamom
½ cup confectioners' sugar
12 tablespoons butter
  (1½ sticks), melted and
  cooled
1 teaspoon vanilla extract
1 teaspoon salt
2 ounces candied citron
Juice and grated peel of
  1 lemon
¾ cup ground almonds
2 cups raisins, soaked in
  warm water and drained
1 egg yolk, slightly beaten

1. Place the yeast, warm milk and 2 tablespoons sugar in a cup or small bowl. Cover and place in a warm place for 10 to 20 minutes, letting the yeast dissolve and rise.
2. In a large bowl, place the 2½ cups flour. Form a "well" in the center of the flour.
3. Add the yeast mixture to the flour.
4. Add the cardamom, confectioners' sugar, butter, vanilla and salt. Combine all the ingredients, forming a soft dough.
5. Fold the citron, lemon juice, lemon peel, almonds and raisins into the dough. Knead for 10 to 15 minutes. Add a little flour to the dough as necessary so that it is not sticky.
6. Form a large ball with the dough. Cover and let it rise in a warm, protected place, until it has doubled in size, about 1 hour.
7. Knead the dough again on a lightly floured surface.
8. With the dough, form 10 to 12 smaller balls. Place the balls on a greased cookie sheet.
9. Mix the egg yolk with a splash of water. Brush the tops of the balls of dough with the egg wash.
10. Bake at 350°F for 30 to 35 minutes, or until golden brown.

Raisin and Nut Cake *Pecivo iz Orehov in Rozin*

This is a wonderful cake, served warm with a good strong cup of coffee in the afternoon. Don't be afraid to serve it with fresh whipped cream. You may substitute fresh berries for the raisins.

Serves 8

Dough:
3 cups all-purpose flour
½ pound (2 sticks) butter,
  softened
½ cup water
½ cup sour cream
Pinch of salt

Filling:
5 eggs, separated
½ cup sugar
½ cup milk
1½ cups sour cream
Grated peel of 1 lemon
⅓ cup all-purpose flour

Topping:
½ cup raisins
½ cup chopped nuts
  (almonds or walnuts)
Confectioners' sugar

1. Mix the ingredients for the dough: 3 cups flour, butter, water, sour cream and pinch of salt, until you have created a soft dough. Add more water, if necessary, to create the right consistency.
2. Cover the dough and place in the refrigerator for ½ hour.
3. Remove the dough from the refrigerator and knead for at least 10 minutes. Roll the dough out on a lightly floured surface until it is a ¾-inch thick circle.
4. Place the dough in a greased pie tin or round baking dish.
5. Bake at 350°F for approximately 15 to 20 minutes, or until very lightly browned.
6. While the dough is baking, mix the ingredients for the filling: 5 egg yolks, sugar, milk, sour cream, lemon rind and flour.
7. Beat the egg whites until stiff. Fold the stiff egg whites into the filling.
8. Remove the dough from the oven before it is well done. Spread the filling on top of the warm dough. Sprinkle the raisins and nuts on top of the filling. Return the cake to the oven and continue baking until the top of the cake is golden brown, 15 to 20 minutes.
9. Remove the cake from the oven. Sprinkle with confectioners' sugar. Serve warm!

Tarragon Cake with Sour Cream

Pehtranova Torta

In Slovenian cooking, it is popular to use fresh herbs to add flavor and variety to baked goods, such as in this tarragon cake. While I was traveling in Slovenia, my car broke down in the town of Radovljica where I was visiting the beekeeping museum. The nearest place for help was a downtown café. When I walked in, I found several older men sitting around drinking beer and eating tarragon cake. Before helping me with my car, they insisted that I join them for a snack. The tarragon cake, although very different to me, was delicious and was a great complement to the cold local beverage.

Serves 12

Dough:
½ pound (2 sticks) butter, softened
2 cups all-purpose flour
1 cup sugar
Grated peel of 1 lemon
2 eggs

Filling:
3 egg yolks (save egg whites for assembly)
1 cup (8 ounces) sour cream
½ cup sugar
½ cup chopped fresh tarragon or 3 tablespoons dried

To Assemble:
1 pound cottage cheese
1 package (1 pound) phyllo dough sheets, thawed
3 tablespoons butter, melted
3 egg whites, slightly beaten

1. Mix together the ingredients for the dough: 2 sticks butter, 2 cups flour, 1 cup sugar, grated lemon peel, 2 eggs.

2. Knead the dough for at least 10 minutes. Place it in the refrigerator for at least 1 hour.

3. In the meantime, mix the filling: 3 egg yolks, sour cream, ½ cup sugar and tarragon.

4. To make the cake, begin by taking the dough out of the refrigerator. Roll it out until it is ½ inch thick. Place in the bottom of a well-greased round baking dish or cake tin.

5. Spread a layer of cottage cheese on the pastry. On top of the cottage cheese, spread a layer of the tarragon mixture.

6. Place a layer of phyllo dough on top of the tarragon filling. Spread with melted butter.

7. Continue building layers until you have filled the tin and have run out of filling.

8. Cover the cake with one last layer of phyllo dough. Brush the top with the slightly beaten egg whites so that it will brown nicely in the oven.

9. Bake at 350°F for 45 minutes, or until nicely browned.

Strudel Štrudel

Strudel is popular in Slovenia, as it is in surrounding Hungary and Austria. Strudels can be sweet, filled with fruit, or savory, filled with spinach or cabbage. It is said that the requirements for a good strudel are a proper dough and a flavorful filling. "Getting a dough that can stretch from Ljubljana to the Danube is the sign of success in making good strudel dough," according to Florence Mirtel of the Slovenian Women's Union of America. Making a proper strudel dough is a difficult, time-consuming task that requires years of experience to get just right. The dough must be stretched quite thinly, and such details as  the humidity in the air and the type of flour used must be considered to get the proper consistency of the dough. The following recipes substitute phyllo pastry sheets for the traditional strudel dough. They are easy to use and provide the perfect texture for a good strudel. Be sure to experiment with your own favorite fillings.

Apple Strudel Jabolčni Štrudel

Serves 6

4 or 5 firm tart apples,
 such as Granny Smith
 or Cortland
Juice of ½ lemon
½ cup sugar
1 teaspoon ground
 cinnamon
1 cup fresh, finely ground
 bread crumbs (optional)
⅔ cup raisins, soaked in
 hot water and drained
 (optional)
6 to 8 sheets phyllo pastry
 dough, thawed
¼ pound (1 stick) butter,
 melted

1. Peel, core and slice the apples (you should end up with 2 to 3 cups of sliced apples).
2. In a small bowl, combine the apples with the lemon juice, sugar and cinnamon. (Add half of the bread crumbs and all of the raisins, if desired.)
3. On a large, clean surface, spread out one of the sheets of phyllo dough.
4. Brush with butter and sprinkle with bread crumbs, if you wish.
5. Place another sheet of dough on top and continue the process until you have 3 or 4 layers of dough prepared.
6. At one of the smaller edges of the rectangular piece of dough, place half of the apple mixture, leaving a few inches of space at the outer edges.
7. Fold the left and right edges of the dough over the apples. Fold the front edge of the dough over the apples, and proceed to roll up the strudel to the far edge of the dough. Brush the top of the strudel with melted butter.
8. In the same manner, make another strudel with the rest of the apple mixture.
9. Place the strudels on a greased cookie sheet. Bake at 350°F for 25 to 30 minutes, or until golden brown.
10. Serve with whipped cream or vanilla ice cream.

Sweet Cheese Strudel *Sirov Štrudel*

Serves 6

1 pound ricotta or cottage
  cheese, drained
1 cup sour cream
2 eggs, beaten
1 teaspoon vanilla extract
1 cup sugar
½ teaspoon salt, or to taste
6 to 8 sheets phyllo pastry
  dough, thawed
¼ pound (1 stick) butter,
  melted
½ cup golden raisins,
  soaked in warm water
  and drained

1. In a bowl, combine the cheese, sour cream, eggs, vanilla, sugar and salt.
2. On a large, clean surface, spread out one of the sheets of phyllo dough. Brush with butter. Place another sheet of dough on top and continue the process until you have 3 or 4 layers of dough prepared.
3. At one of the smaller edges of the rectangular piece of dough, place half of the cheese mixture, leaving a few inches of space at the outer edges.
4. Sprinkle half of the raisins on the cheese.
5. Fold the left and right edges of the dough, over the cheese. Fold the front edge of the dough, and proceed to roll up the strudel to the far edge of the dough. Brush the top of the strudel with melted butter.
6. In the same manner, make another strudel with the rest of the cheese mixture.
7. Place the strudels on a greased cookie sheet. Bake at 350°F for 30 to 40 minutes, or until golden brown.

Sour Cherry Strudel Češnjev Štrudel

Serves 6

2 to 3 cups pitted cherries
½ cup sugar
1 teaspoon ground
  cinnamon
1 cup fine, sweet bread
  crumbs
½ cup finely chopped
  walnuts (optional)
6 to 8 sheets phyllo pastry
  dough, thawed
¼ pound (1 stick) butter,
  melted

1. Follow the recipe for apple strudel, page 178, eliminating the lemon juice and substituting the cherries for the apples. If you wish, add chopped walnuts to the cherry mixture.

Cabbage Strudel Zeljev Zavitek

Serves 4 to 6

1 head fresh cabbage
½ cup olive oil
1 medium onion,
  peeled and thinly sliced
2 teaspoons salt
Freshly ground pepper
½ teaspoon caraway seeds
  (optional)
6 to 8 sheets phyllo pastry
  dough, thawed

1. Wash and core the cabbage, removing the outer leaves. Slice the cabbage thinly.
2. In a large skillet, heat 2 to 3 tablespoons of the oil. Place the cabbage, onion, salt, pepper, and caraway seeds, if desired, into the pan.
3. Cook and stir the cabbage and onion until the cabbage is softened. Remove from the heat and let cool.
4. Lay out a sheet of phyllo dough. Brush with oil. Continue to add phyllo sheets until you have 3 to 4 layers brushed with oil.
5. Place half of the cabbage mixture at one end of the sheets of dough. Fold and roll the strudel as in the apple strudel recipe on page 178. Repeat.
6. Place the strudels on a greased cookie sheet. Bake at 350°F for 30 to 35 minutes, or until golden brown.

Spinach Strudel Špinačni Štrudel

1 pound fresh spinach, or 1-pound package frozen spinach, thawed
½ cup olive oil
1 medium onion, peeled and chopped
1 clove garlic, peeled and chopped
1 pound ricotta cheese
4 eggs
1 teaspoon salt
Freshly ground pepper
½ teaspoon grated nutmeg
6 to 8 sheets phyllo pastry dough, thawed

1. If you are using fresh spinach, wash the leaves and remove the stems. Steam the spinach. Drain and let cool. Chop the cooked spinach. If you are using frozen spinach, defrost and drain the spinach. Cut into small pieces.

2. In a skillet, heat 2 to 3 tablespoons of the olive oil. Cook and stir the onion, garlic and spinach for 6 to 8 minutes, or until the onion has softened. Remove from heat and let cool.

3. In a large bowl, combine the spinach mixture with the ricotta cheese, eggs, salt, pepper and nutmeg.

4. Lay out a sheet of phyllo dough. Brush with oil. Continue to add phyllo sheets until you have 3 to 4 layers brushed with oil.

5. Place half of the spinach mixture at one end of the sheets of dough. Fold and roll the strudel as in the apple strudel recipe on page 178. Repeat.

6. Bake at 350°F for 30 to 35 minutes, or until golden brown.

ther
Desserts

To the Poet
Pevcu

Who'll say
How to brighten dark night, which the soul
    can dismay!

Who'll free
Himself from the heart-piercing hawk's agony
From morning to dusk and through nightly
    ennui?

Who'll try
To wipe from his mem'ry the days now gone
    by,
Remove all tomorrow's despair from his eye,
And from today's smoth'ring emptiness fly!

You'll know
The life of a poet, it brings too much woe
Either heav'n or hell through thy bosom must
    flow!

Anew
Recall your vocation, endure it with rue!

– France Prešeren
Translated by Tom Priestly and
Henry Cooper

Crêpes Palačinke

Crêpes with a variety of fillings or sauces are popular for dessert in Slovenia.

Makes approximately twelve 7-inch crêpes

2 eggs, slightly beaten
1 cup milk
½ teaspoon salt
1 cup all-purpose flour
2 tablespoons butter,
  melted
Butter or oil, for frying

1. To make the crêpe batter, mix the eggs, milk, salt, flour and butter until a smooth batter is formed. Let it sit for a few minutes.
2. In a small skillet or omelet pan, melt a teaspoon of butter or oil over medium to high heat.
3. Pour a few tablespoons of the batter into the heated pan. Tilt the pan and swirl the batter so that it covers the bottom of the pan evenly, and a nice round crêpe is formed. Cook for 3 to 4 minutes, or until the edges have browned.
4. Flip the crêpe over to cook on the other side. Cook for another 2 to 3 minutes, or until the other side is nicely browned.
5. Continue to make crêpes until the batter is gone. Keep the crêpes covered in a warm oven until you are ready to use them. You may also reheat them later. Crêpes also freeze well. Stack them layered with wax paper or paper towels, and cover them well before putting them into the freezer.

Crêpes with Vanilla Ice Cream and Chocolate Sauce

Palačinke z Vanilijevim Sladoledom in Čokoladnim Prelivom

Serves 8

Chocolate Sauce:
2 tablespoons butter
2 squares (1 ounce each) unsweetened chocolate
1 cup sugar
½ cup milk or water
Pinch of salt
1½ teaspoons vanilla extract

8 crêpes (see recipe page 184)
8 large scoops vanilla ice cream
Fresh whipped cream (optional)
Chopped nuts (optional)

1. To make the chocolate sauce, in a saucepan melt the butter and chocolate. Slowly stir in the sugar and milk. Add the salt and vanilla. Continue to stir over low heat until you have a thick sauce.
2. Heat the crêpes in the oven at low heat, or reheat them briefly in the skillet.
3. Place a few scoops of ice cream in each crêpe and roll them up.
4. Serve topped with chocolate sauce and whipped cream and chopped nuts, if you wish.

Crêpes with Walnuts and Frothy Wine Sauce Palačinke Vinski Sadó

Makes 8 crêpes

8 prepared crêpes (from recipe on page 184)

Filling:
1 cup walnuts, finely chopped
¼ cup sugar, or to taste
1 teaspoon ground cinnamon

Wine Sauce (Vinski Sadó):
4 egg yolks
1 tablespoon freshly squeezed lemon juice
¼ cup sugar
1 cup sweet white dessert wine

1. To make the filling for the crêpes, mix the walnuts, sugar and cinnamon.
2. Take a warm crêpe and spread half of it with the nut mixture. Loosely roll the crêpe up, or fold in half. Repeat until the crêpes and the nut mixture have been used up.
3. To make the wine sauce, beat together the egg yolks, lemon juice and sugar. Continue beating, and slowly add the white wine.
4. Heat the wine sauce over a double boiler, beating it continuously, until the sauce is frothy.
5. When it is done, pour the sauce over the crêpes that have been filled with the nut mixture. Serve immediately.

Baked Apples with Cranberries Pečena Jabolka z Brusnicami

Serves 4

4 large apples
¼ cup fresh cranberry sauce (see recipe on page 212)
2 eggs, separated
½ cup ground almonds
¼ cup fresh, sweet bread crumbs
¼ cup sugar
2 cups red wine
Grated peel of 1 lemon
4 whole cloves
2 cinnamon sticks, broken into pieces
2 tablespoons butter

Topping:
1 pint heavy whipping cream
½ teaspoon vanilla extract
2 teaspoons sugar

1. Peel and core each apple, without making a hole at the bottom.
2. Place approximately 1 tablespoon of cranberry sauce at the bottom of each apple core.
3. Mix together the egg yolks, almonds, bread crumbs, and sugar. Beat the egg whites until they are stiff. Fold into the almond mixture.
4. Fill the rest of the apples with the filling, mounding it on top, if you have too much filling.
5. Place the stuffed apples in a baking dish. Pour the red wine over the apples. Add the lemon peel, cloves and cinnamon sticks to the pan, and dot the apples with the butter.
6. Bake the apples at 350°F for about 1 hour, basting the apples with the wine and juices every 10 minutes.
7. To make the whipped cream topping, beat the cream, vanilla and sugar with an electric mixer. Mix at high speed until the whipped cream is thick.
8. Serve the apples hot with some of their own juices, and topped with the whipped cream.

Baked Fresh Figs with Vanilla Ice Cream Sveže Pečene Fige z Vanilijevim Sladoledom

For this tasty dessert, you may also use fresh plums, pears or peaches, if fresh figs are unavailable.

Serves 4

8 fresh figs (or two per person)
2 to 3 tablespoons sugar (optional)
1 cup vanilla ice cream

1. Wash the fruit and cut them in half. If you are using plums or peaches, remove the pits.
2. Place the fruit, skin side down, on a cookie sheet.
3. Sprinkle with sugar, if desired.
4. Bake the fruit at 325°F for 20 to 25 minutes, or until the fruit is slightly roasted, but not dried out.
5. Remove from the oven. Place the fruit on a dessert plate. Top with vanilla ice cream.

Chocolate Torte Čokolada Torta

Serves 8

Cake:
Grated rind of 1 lemon
1 cup sugar
8 eggs
1½ cups all-purpose flour

Frosting:
6 ounces semi-sweet
  chocolate (chocolate
  chips or squares)
½ pound butter (2 sticks)
2 cups confectioners' sugar
1 egg
1½ tablespoons vanilla
  extract
1 cup finely ground
  hazelnuts or pecans

1. To make the cake, combine the lemon peel, sugar and eggs. Beat with an electric mixer for 10 to 15 minutes, until the batter is thick and smooth.

2. Slowly add the flour to the batter, beating continuously with the electric mixer.

3. Grease the bottom of two or three 8-inch round cake pans. (Traditionally, beeswax is used to coat the bottom of the pan. You may use butter or oil.)

4. Fill the cake pans with ⅙ of the cake batter. (You will be baking 6 layers of cake.)

5. Bake the cakes at 325°F for about 20 minutes, or until the cake is done when tested with a toothpick.

6. Remove the cakes from the pans and allow to cool. Continue baking the cake layers until the batter is gone, and you have 6 layers of cake.

7. To make the frosting, heat the chocolate over a double boiler, or over low heat. When the chocolate is soft, add the butter to the pan. Continue to heat until the chocolate and butter are soft.

8. In a bowl, combine the chocolate and butter with the sugar, egg and vanilla.

9. Spread the frosting on each layer of cake, saving enough frosting for the top and the sides. Stack the cake layers on top of each other. Frost the top of the cake and the sides. Sprinkle with the ground nuts.

Grape Torte *Grozdje v Testu* ●———

Serves 8

Pastry:
1 cup all-purpose flour
¼ teaspoon salt
¼ pound (1 stick) butter, cut into small pieces
1 egg yolk
3 tablespoons ice water, or as needed

Filling:
6 tablespoons butter, softened
¼ cup sugar, plus 2 tablespoons
3 eggs, separated
¼ teaspoon salt
2 tablespoons kirschwasser or fruit brandy
1 teaspoon grated lemon rind
1 pound seedless grapes (green, red or a combination), washed, dried, and cut in half

Confectioners' sugar for sprinkling

1. To make the pastry, combine the flour and salt in a large bowl. Cut the butter into the flour using two knives, forks, or a pastry blender, until the mixture looks like coarse meal.

2. In a small bowl, whisk together the egg yolk and water. Add this to the flour mixture, combining until you have formed a smooth dough, or you can form a ball with the dough.

3. Cover the dough with wax paper or plastic wrap and refrigerate for at least 20 minutes.

4. Butter a pie dish or a round springform pan. When you are ready to use the dough, roll it out onto a floured surface until it reaches the size that you need to cover the bottom and the sides of the baking dish, or you may pat the dough into the pan using your fingers. Prick the dough on the bottom of the baking dish with a fork.

5. For the filling, mix the softened butter with ¼ cup sugar. Use an electric mixer in order to create a soft, fluffy mixture. Add the egg yolks, mixing continuously. Continue beating and add the salt, kirschwasser and lemon rind.

6. In a separate bowl and with clean beaters, beat the egg whites with the 2 tablespoons of sugar until fluffy and stiff. Fold the egg white mixture into the egg yolk mixture.

7. Pour the egg mixture onto the bottom of the pastry dough.

8. Arrange the grape halves on top, pressing them slightly into the batter. You may place them skin side up, or down, as you wish. You may also place them on their sides. Be creative.

9. Bake the torte at 375°F for 45 minutes to 1 hour, or until the pastry crust is golden brown. **10.** Remove from the oven and allow to cool. When the torte is completely cooled, you may remove the sides of the springform pan, if you have used one. Before serving, sprinkle with confectioners' sugar.

Nut Torte _Lešnikova Torta_

Serves 10

Cake:
1½ cups all-purpose flour
¾ cup sugar
4 eggs
⅓ cup cocoa, powdered

Frosting:
12 tablespoons butter
  (1½ sticks), softened
1 cup confectioners' sugar
1 cup finely chopped
  almonds
½ cup powdered cocoa
2 eggs
2 tablespoons granulated
  sugar
2 tablespoons cornstarch
2 tablespoons water, or as
  needed
Splash of milk
Splash of rum

Topping:
5 squares (1-ounce each)
  semisweet chocolate
Splash of milk
⅓ cup chopped almonds

1. For the cake, combine the flour, sugar, eggs and cocoa. Mix well. You may use an electric beater to prepare a smooth batter.

2. Grease either a 9-inch round springform pan, or 3 smaller 9-inch or 8-inch cake pans. Pour the batter into the pans. (All of it into the large pan, or ⅓ of the batter into each of the smaller cake pans.)

3. Bake the cake at 350°F: the larger cake for 45 minutes; the smaller cakes for 20 minutes. Test with a toothpick to make sure they are done. Remove from the oven and let cool. When the cakes are cool, remove from the baking pans.

4. To make the frosting, beat together with an electric mixer the butter, confectioners' sugar and almonds. Continue to mix and add the cocoa, eggs, and granulated sugar. In a small bowl, whisk together the cornstarch and water. Add to the frosting. Add the milk and rum, and continue to mix until you have created a smooth frosting.

5. Cut the larger cake into 3 layers, or use the smaller cakes for the layers. Spread ⅓ of the frosting on top of one of the 3 cakes. Place the second cake on top of that. Continue to frost the layers until you have 3 layers of cake and frosting.

6. To prepare the chocolate coating, melt the chocolate in a double boiler. Stir in the milk to make it creamy.

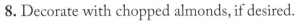

7. Pour the chocolate on top of the cake. Smooth it with a cake knife, making sure to cover the sides of the cake.

8. Decorate with chopped almonds, if desired.

Note: Frosting contains raw eggs.

Crème Caramel <small>Rožata</small>

Serves 4

4 tablespoons (½ stick)
  butter, softened
2 cups sugar
1 quart milk
2 teaspoons vanilla extract
Pinch of salt
Grated peel from 1 lemon
8 eggs

1. Before preparing the custard, prepare the molds. Using either 4 small custard dishes or 1 large one, butter each dish.

2. In a saucepan, heat ½ cup of the sugar, stirring continuously, until the sugar has browned and a caramel sauce has formed.

3. Quickly, while it is still liquid, pour the caramel sauce into each mold, covering the bottom of each dish, and the sides, if possible.

4. To prepare the custard, in a saucepan, heat the milk, vanilla, remaining 1½ cups of sugar, salt and lemon rind over low heat. Cook it slightly for 5 to 6 minutes, while stirring; do not allow it to boil. Remove from the heat.

5. In a bowl, beat the eggs until they are frothy. Mix the eggs with the warmed milk.

6. Pour the mixture through a sieve and into another bowl.

7. Quickly pour the custard into the prepared custard dishes.

8. Place the custard dishes in a large baking pan and fill the pan halfway with water.

9. Bake the custard at 350°F for 45 minutes, or until a skewer or toothpick comes out clean when inserted.

10. Remove from oven. Allow to cool for 10 minutes. Refrigerate the custard before serving.

Layered Cake with Apples and Walnuts Gibanica

As with potica, there are many versions of this hearty, layered cake in Slovenia: savory ones with cottage cheese or buckwheat, and sweet versions with raisins and nuts. This sweet version of gibanica is from the Prekmurja region of Slovenia, and was given to me by Marina Kristanc, the head chef of the restaurant at the Grand Hotel Toplice in Bled. The cake is made with layers of dough and several types of fillings: a "sweet lasagna." Although it is time consuming to make, the result is a beautiful work of art. The traditional versions of the recipe call for you to make your own sheets of pastry. Marina recommends using prepared phyllo dough.

Serves 10

8 or 10 sheets phyllo pastry
¾ cup poppy seeds
1 cup milk
2 or 3 small apples, peeled, cored, and sliced thinly
½ cup raisins, soaked in warm water or rum, and drained
½ cup sugar
1 teaspoon vanilla extract
1 teaspoon ground cinnamon
Grated rind and juice of 1 lemon
1½ pounds cottage or ricotta cheese
2 eggs
1 cup sour cream
1 cup chopped walnuts
4 tablespoons (½ stick) butter, melted
Confectioners' sugar, for sprinkling

1. If you are using frozen phyllo, defrost the dough slowly by putting it in the refrigerator overnight, or follow the directions on the package.

2. Boil the poppy seeds in 1 cup milk for 20 to 25 minutes. Once the poppy seeds have softened, remove them from the heat and drain. Let cool.

3. Prepare the first filling for the gibanica: In a medium bowl, combine the apples, raisins, sugar, vanilla, cinnamon, lemon rind and juice.

4. Prepare the second filling for the gibanica: In a medium bowl, combine the cottage or ricotta cheese with the eggs and sour cream.

5. Working carefully so as not to break the dough, lay one phyllo sheet in the bottom of a large, greased rectangular baking pan. Brush lightly with melted butter. Place a second sheet on top of the first, brush with more butter. (Make sure the rest of the phyllo sheets are covered so that they do not dry out.)

6. Spread a layer of the cottage cheese mixture over the phyllo.

7. Cover with another sheet of phyllo and brush with butter.

8. Spread a layer of the raisin and apple mixture over the phyllo.

9. Sprinkle a layer of walnuts and poppy seeds.

10. Continue layer by layer to build the cake, until all of the ingredients are used. Make sure the cake is covered with 2 phyllo sheets. Brush the top with butter.

11. Bake at 300°F for 1½ to 2 hours, until golden brown on top.

12. Remove from oven and sprinkle with confectioners' sugar. Serve warm with a cup of coffee or a dry white wine such as a Beli Pinot.

Chestnut Cream Kostanjeva Krema

Serves 6

1 pound chestnuts, peeled (see page 99 for how to peel chestnuts)
2 cups milk
Pinch of salt
¾ cup granulated sugar
½ teaspoon vanilla extract
½ cup whipping cream
2 tablespoons powdered cocoa
2 tablespoons cognac or rum (optional)
Confectioners' sugar, to taste
Toasted almonds for garnish (optional)

1. Place the peeled chestnuts in a large saucepan. Add the milk, salt, sugar and vanilla. Heat over medium to high heat, and bring to a boil. Reduce to medium heat and simmer for 20 to 30 minutes, or until the chestnuts are very soft and beginning to fall apart. (You may add more milk, if necessary, to make sure there is enough liquid to cook the chestnuts.)

2. Remove the chestnuts from the heat. Drain them, keeping the milk in which they were cooked.

3. Once the chestnuts have cooled, process them in a food processor. Add the whipping cream, cocoa, and cognac. Also add a few tablespoons of the reserved milk, or as much as is necessary to produce a smooth cream.

4. Taste the chestnut cream. Add confectioners' sugar, as desired, to sweeten.

5. Refrigerate the cream for several hours. Serve topped with sweetened whipped cream and toasted almonds, if desired.

Fruit Tart *Sadni Kolač*

Fruit tarts are a sweet treat in Slovenia. Use any fresh fruit that is in season: strawberries, raspberries, blueberries, peaches, or a combination of all four.

Serves 8

Crust:
½ cup finely chopped
  almonds
12 tablespoons butter
  (1½ sticks), cut into
  cubes
1½ cups all-purpose flour
⅓ cup sugar
Grated rind of 1 lemon
1 egg, slightly beaten
1 teaspoon vanilla extract

Vanilla Cream:
3 egg yolks
4 tablespoons sugar
2 tablespoons all-purpose
  flour
1 teaspoon vanilla extract
1½ cups milk
Splash of rum or cognac

Fruit Topping:
1 pound fresh fruit (about
  4 cups)
1 cup red currant jelly
1 package (¼ ounce)
  unflavored gelatin
¼ cup cognac or Grand
  Marnier (optional)

1. To make the crust, crumble together the almonds, butter, flour, sugar, lemon rind, egg and vanilla. Set aside in a cool place to let it rest for 1 to 2 hours.

2. Put the dough out on a floured surface. Knead it for a few minutes, and roll it out. Cut it the size of a shallow tart pan. Butter the bottom of the pan, and place the dough tightly in the bottom and up the sides of the pan.

3. Preheat the oven to 400°F. Place the crust in the oven. Bake for approximately 20 minutes.

4. Remove the crust from the oven, allow it to cool.

5. To make the vanilla cream, combine the egg yolks, sugar, flour, vanilla and some of the cold milk in a saucepan. Cook over medium heat, stirring continuously. Warm the remaining milk. Slowly add the warm milk to the cream. Whisk continuously over the heat until creamy and smooth.

6. Spread the vanilla cream on the cooled crust.

7. Wash, dry and slice the fruit. Arrange it on top of the cream.

8. For the topping, in a small saucepan, heat the jelly, gelatin and cognac, stirring continuously.

9. While it is still warm, pour it over the fruit. Allow to cool.

10. Slice the tart and serve with whipped cream or vanilla ice cream.

Sem dolgo upal in se bal,
Slovó sem upu, strahu dal;
Srcé je prazno, srečno ni,
Nazaj si up in strah želi.

In hope, in dread long did I dwell.
To hope and fear I said farewell.
My heart, now empty, holds no cheer,
It yearns again for hope and fear.

– France Prešeren, from the introduction to
Poezije Doktorja Franceta Prešerna
Translated by Tom Priestly

FRANCE PREŠEREN: A NATIONAL POET

In the first half of the nineteenth century, Slovenians and several other ethnic groups found themselves under the rule of the Austro-Hungarian Empire. Between 1814 and 1848, there was a wave of intense literary and cultural activity, that gave rise to a romantic Slovenian nationalistic movement. Slovenians longed for the unity of all historic Slovenian lands. Although they remained under Austrian rule, they demanded political freedom, Slovene schools, a Slovenian university, Slovenian laws, and a Slovenian flag and seal. During this time, censorship was removed by the Hungarians, and Slovenian plays, poems, and newspapers were able to thrive in several Slovenian dialects. The poet France Prešeren played a large role in this nationalistic revival. His poems–epic, romantic, sonnets, satire, and mature verse– have inspired Slovenes for generations, and continue to do so to this day. He published a volume of his works in Slovenian in 1846, at a time when German was the literary language, establishing a voice for Slovenes in the world of European poetry. When Slovenians voted to establish an independent republic in 1990, they turned to France Prešeren's works for the words to their new national anthem.

Prešeren was born in the peasant village of Vrba near Bled in 1800. He was one of eight children, and, being the smartest of the bunch, was sent away for special schooling. He studied law in Vienna and became an attorney employed by law firms. When he became frustrated working for others, he tried to establish his own law practice in Kranj. He died an untimely death in 1849 before he was able to do so.

Prešeren began writing poetry in the 1820s when he was studying in Vienna. In the 1830s, his public career started with the publishing of his works in the newly established Slovenian literary journal, *The Krajnska čbelica* (*The Carniolan Bee*), which was made possible by the promotion of his works by his best friend and literary mentor, Marija Čop, a librarian and teacher of modest means. Prešeren's works were popular immediately, partly because they were considered scandalous. But more important, Prešeren and Čop promoted a certain approach to Slovenian nationalism.

Slovenia is too small, they concluded, to fight the external pressures of conquering forces, be they religious, political, or cultural. To survive these pressures, Slovenia must accommodate itself to these forces, while choosing the best of them. Ancient traditions may need to give way to new ones, but innovations need to be "Slovenized." Only in this way, could their nation absorb change, and maintain their identity at the same time. Prešeren and Čop applied this lesson to the absorption of 1830s romantic literary culture in Slovenia. It is a lesson that applied as well during the changes in Slovenia in the second half of the nineteenth century. In one of his works, Prešeren made the mistake of referring to a young woman with whom he was smitten. The young woman was far above him socially, and for his attraction, her family banned him from Ljubljana society altogether. Prešeren was known to drink a lot, and to chase women much younger than himself, fathering several illegitimate children. He became an outcast in conservative Ljubljana society.

In the 1830s, Prešeren lost many friends, including Marija Čop, who died in a drowning accident. He became quite depressed and became a recluse. Although his productivity dropped off during this time, it was also a time that he produced some of his best-known works. The epic poem "The Baptism under the Savica" marked the death of his close friend. The poem also incorporated nationalism, and is considered to be autobiographical. In it, frustrated at every turn in life, Prešeren concludes that there is no such thing as true happiness here on earth.

Although his approach to life was somewhat grim, Prešeren wrote in a variety of styles and on many topics. He wrote clever poems in structured verse ("The Poet"), lighthearted poems ("The Toast"), poems with a darker tone ("The Unwed Mother"), and romantic ballads, with the continual theme of love gone wrong. He wrote sonnets ("The Wreath of Sonnets") and reworked traditional folk tales ("Lovely Vida"). In ill health and dispirited, he died an untimely death on February 8, 1849. It seemed that he and his works would be forgotten. However, in the second half of the nineteenth century, his works were rediscovered. Although Prešeren remains unknown outside of Slovenia, he is considered a real Slovenian hero, and is truly a "national poet."

A picture of the poet France Prešeren is proudly displayed on the Slovenian currency, here shown on the 1,000 Tolar note.

THE UNWED MOTHER
Nezakonska Mati

What need for you was ever there,
Child so dear, child so fair?
I am young, by fate mislead
I, a mother, never wed.

By father I was cured and strapped,
And bitterly my mother wept;
My own were overcome with shame,
The rest could only point in blame.

He who was my heart's delight
Whom your father name by right,
Disappeared to parts unnamed,
For we made him so ashamed!

What need for you was ever there,
Child so dear, child so fair?
But whether there was need or no,
With all my heart I love you so.

I see the sky before me rise
Whene'er I look into your eyes,
And when I see your lovely smile,
All my pain seems well worthwhile.

May you joyful days be giv'n
By Him who made the birds of heav'n,
And whether there is need or no.
With all my heart I'll love you so.

– France Prešeren
Translated by Tom Priestly and
Henry Cooper

THE COUNTRY OF CASTLES

Slovenia, once known as "the country of castles," had at one time as many as one thousand castles. Many of these castles were originally built in the thirteenth century as protection against invading Turks. In later years, they were restored or rebuilt to become manors for barons and baronesses. Many of these castles have been destroyed over the years by wars or as the result of development. However, many beautiful ones remain today and can be visited by the public. In many cases, the castles provide historic and beautiful settings for hotels, restaurants, and recreational activities.

Bled Castle, high above Lake Bled in the Bohinj region, may be the most photographed castle in Slovenia. It is a typical medieval fort complete with ramparts, towers, and a moat. The original building dates back to the eleventh century, but most of the building standing today was built in the sixteenth century. A short hike up the cliff from the lake, the castle is on two levels. The terrace on the upper level overlooking the lake and the nearby mountains has a breathtaking view, and is the site of many weddings and celebrations. The castle is open to the public and offers a museum, chapel, and restaurant.

Otočec Castle is on a tiny island in the middle of the Krka River in Otočec, in the Dolenjska region. It is one of the loveliest and most complete castles in Slovenia. One approaches Otočec Castle over a drawbridge connecting the castle to the mainland. In recent years, it has been turned into a luxury hotel. In the courtyard, a lovely restaurant and café offer anyone the chance to sit and enjoy the late-Gothic and Renaissance architecture. Nearby on the mainland portion of Otočec, one can enjoy tennis, mountain biking, horseback riding, camping, canoeing, fishing, and a steam bath and sauna spa.

Mokrice Castle, located in Brežice near the Croatian border, was built in the sixteenth century, although remnants date back to Roman times. The coat of arms of Mokrice depicts a raven with an arrow shot through its throat. It is said that a Turkish soldier shot the raven as it was about to warn the castle inhabitants of approaching troops. The castle now houses the Mokrice Castle Golf Hotel, complete with luxury rooms, a courtyard for special events, and an excellent restaurant featuring high-end Slovenian wines. On the grounds of the castle are pear tree orchards, English gardens with rare plants, and a riding stable. The location also features Mokrice Golf Course. This hilly and difficult eighteen-hole course runs through the former hunting grounds of the castle, and the tenth hole is a short par three where the castle moat used to be.

Ljubljana Castle sits high above the capital city on "castle hill." There has been some type of fortress at this location since Celtic times, but the current structure was built in the sixteenth century, after the earthquake in 1511. From the castle are beautiful views of the city below and the surrounding valleys. The castle is often used for such events as concerts and weddings. One can walk over the ramparts and climb to the top of the castle tower. The ceiling in the chapel built in 1489 is covered with frescoes and depicts the coat of arms of the dukes of Carniola.

Predjama Castle has probably the most dramatic setting of any castle in Slovenia. Located near Postojna, the castle sits at the entrance of a large cavern, halfway up a steep hillside. This four-story castle was built in the sixteenth century, although parts of the structure date back to the thirteenth century. The castle has many legends attached to it, but the best-known is that of the fifteenth-century rebel, Erazem Lueger. (See "The Legend of Erazem Lueger: A Slovenian Robin Hood," page 120.) The castle provides dramatic views of the surrounding valley, and it has a drawbridge over a raging river, holes in the walls of the entrance tower for pouring boiling oil on invaders, and a dark and dank dungeon. The castle museum includes portraits of Erazem, and a sixteenth-century chest full of treasure, which was unearthed at the castle in 1991.

THE SOČA (ISONZO) FRONT AND THE WAR TO END ALL WARS

Kobarid and the Soča Valley are in one of the most beautiful areas of northwestern Slovenia. Located in the mountains near the Italian border, it is also the location of one of the longest and most tragic battles of World War I. Described in Ernest Hemingway's *A Farewell to Arms*, the Soča Front (Caporetto in Italian) cost the lives of hundreds of thousands of soldiers, and, together with civilians, ended in the loss of almost one million people. Hemingway was injured during this battle while driving an ambulance.

In May 1915, Italy declared war on the Central Powers and moved its army to the strategically important Soča Valley. The Italians hoped to travel through the valley, making their way to Austro-Hungary. However, the Austrians had fortified their eighty kilometer line, stretching from the Adriatic Sea to the mountains. The first Italian offensive was successful, and they occupied Kobarid. They soon reached a stalemate, and remained stuck in the mountains for twenty-nine months. The battle turned into a war of attrition, as the difficult mountain terrain helped to entrench the two armies. The fighting was horrible, the climate difficult, and neither army made progress until October 1917. The Austrians organized a surprise attack, moving hundreds of troops surreptitiously. In the battle of October 24, 1917, "the miracle of Kobarid," the Austrian army pushed the Italians to the

Friulian Plain. The fighting continued there for one more year.

The sketches and drawings of German Lieutenant Erwin Rommel (known later as the "Desert Fox") were invaluable for understanding this complex and strategic move by the Central Powers. A museum dedicated to this battle was established in Kobarid in 1990. Housing hundreds of photographs, diaries, and other WWI memorabilia, the museum has received several European awards.

An old postcard depicting the battle in the Soča Valley.

Sauces and Drinks

Vino lep poje, pleše in gode, a nerado dela.
Wine plays, sings, and dances well, but doesn't
like to work.

– Slovenian proverb

Horseradish Hren

Fresh horseradish can be used as a side dish for meats and sausages, or in sauces. You may prepare large batches of freshly grated horseradish at a time. Store it, well covered or in glass jars, in the refrigerator. Once you get used to freshly grated horseradish, it will be difficult for you to use the prepared, store-bought versions!

Makes approximately 2 cups

1 horseradish root (about ½ pound)
1 to 2 teaspoons salt
½ cup vinegar, or as needed

1. Peel the horseradish root.
2. Grate the horseradish into a large bowl.
3. Add salt and vinegar and combine the ingredients.
4. Make sure that all of the horseradish is covered with vinegar. Add more vinegar as necessary, otherwise the horseradish will turn brown.
5. Cover well, or put in glass jars, and refrigerate.

Pepper and Eggplant Relish Ajvar

Ajvar is a flavorful relish that can be served as an appetizer with crackers or bread, or as a side dish with grilled meats. Ajvar goes especially well with čevapčiči (see page 148). Ajvar has its roots in Turkish cuisine, reflecting the Balkan influence on Central European culture, and Slovenians have developed their own recipes. In Kosovo or Albania, for example, Ajvar is made with chile peppers and can be quite spicy. Further north, such as in Slovenia or Croatia, sweet peppers are used, creating a milder relish. It is often prepared by households in late summer or early fall, when peppers are harvested from vegetable gardens. Large quantities of ajvar are prepared at once and placed in jars that are then stored and used over the winter months.

Makes 2 or 3 jars

2 medium eggplants
3 green bell peppers
3 red bell peppers (include
　chile peppers, if you wish,
　for more heat)
3 or 4 large cloves garlic,
　peeled and minced
½ cup olive oil
Juice of 1 lemon
Salt
Freshly ground pepper
Fresh parsley, chopped
　(optional)

1. Preheat the oven to 375°F. Place the eggplants and peppers on a cookie sheet. Bake them in the preheated oven until they are tender when pierced with a fork, and the skins are blackened and blistered.
2. Remove from the oven and place the roasted vegetables in a brown paper bag. Close the bag, and let the vegetables steam in their own heat for 10 to 15 minutes. This will make the skins easier to remove.
3. Peel the eggplants and the peppers. Remove the stems and seeds. Chop the vegetables into small pieces. (The eggplant will be mushy.)
4. In a large bowl, combine the vegetables with the garlic, olive oil and lemon juice. Season with salt and pepper, to taste.
5. Sprinkle with the parsley, if so desired.
6. Store in the refrigerator well covered, or in sealed glass jars.

Cranberry Sauce Omaka iz Brusnic

Serve this sauce with venison dishes or meat dumplings.

**Makes approximately
2 cups**

**1 bag (12 ounce)
  fresh cranberries**
1 cup sugar
1 cup water
Grated zest of 1 orange

1. In a medium saucepan, combine all of the ingredients.
2. Cook over high heat until the mixture boils. Continue to cook at high heat for about 10 minutes, or until the cranberries pop.
3. Remove any foam that has risen to the top. Remove the cranberries from the heat and allow to cool.
4. Store in a tightly sealed container. You may also freeze this sauce!

SLOVENIAN WINES

Slovenia's unique location at the foot of the Alps, the edge of the Mediterranean Sea and the beginning of the Pannonian plains creates a wonderful climate for growing grapes. Vines have been cultivated in Slovenia for thousands of years, the first vines planted by the Celts. The Romans improved upon the local viticulture, taking advantage of the soil and diverse climactic conditions.

Today there are almost twenty-two thousand hectares of vineyards in Slovenia producing between 60 to 70 million bottles of wine annually. Some Slovenian wine is exported but the best wines, often produced in small vineyards, are found only in Slovenia.

There are fifteen wine-making districts in Slovenia in three main wine-growing regions: Primorska, or coastal region; Posavje, in the Sava Valley; and Podravje in the Drava Valley. In all, more than 120 vineyards produce hundreds of types of wines.

The coastal region, Primorska, is known for its whites and reds. A typical white wine of the region is the yellowy Malvazija, which is a wonderful complement to seafood. The reds from the coast include Teran, made from the Slovenian Refošk grape, which goes well with game and prosciutto. A red merlot, Vipavski Merlot, from the Vipava Valley, is also popular.

The Posavje region in southern Slovenia is known for its Cviček, a dry, light red which is very much Slovenian. It is similar to a

French rosé. Podravje, in the northeast, produces more whites such as a Renski Rizling (a German Riesling), Beli Pinot (white pinot) and Traminec (traminer). A variety of vineyards produce wonderful Chardonnays, Cabernet Sauvignon, and muškat, to name a few. Slovenian sparkling wine is also popular and some of the best is produced by Zlata Radganska Penina and Barbara International. Slovenian wines have a labeling system according to the quality of the wine. *Vrhunsko vino*, premium wine, has a gold label; *kakovostno vino*, quality wine, a silver label; and *namizno vino*, table wine, a bronze label. There is also *archivsko vino*, or archive wine, which is considered the highest quality. One can make a *vinska cesta*, or wine tour, in the winemaking regions. These roads, which one can follow with a car or a bicycle, lead through the major vineyards. Along the way, one can also stop at a *klet* (cellar) for wine tasting. Some are well-organized, in the style of Napa Valley; others are smaller and more low key, and one will end up discussing the wine with the local farmer (in Slovenian, of course).

In Slovenia, wine can be purchased at a *vinoteka* (a wine store), a grocery store, or even a convenience store at a highway gas station. It is always served with meals, and in many Slovenian restaurants you may purchase a jug of the local wine, as well as select a bottle from their wine list.

Dandelion Wine Domače Regratovo Vino

2 pounds dandelion
  blossoms
2 quarts boiling water
3 lemons
4 oranges
3 pounds sugar
Warm water, as needed
1 cake (2 ounce) fresh yeast

1. When selecting the dandelion blossoms, choose the ones that are in full bloom.

2. Wash the flowers and remove the stems.

3. Place the blossoms in a large pan. Cover with the boiling water.

4. Cover the pan with a clean cloth and let stand for 24 hours.

5. Clean and dry a large 2-gallon jug or crock.

6. Pour the liquid into the crock through a strainer, removing all the flowers. Squeeze each of the blossoms dry before throwing them away.

7. Wash, dry and quarter each of the lemons and oranges. Squeeze the juice of each fruit into the dandelion liquid and add the rinds.

8. Add the sugar to the liquid, stirring until it dissolves.

9. Add enough warm water to make the mixture 1 gallon.

10. Crumble the fresh yeast into the liquid. Cover the crock with a clean cloth.

11. For 5 days, stir the liquid twice daily, in the morning and in the evening.

12. Cover the crock loosely. Let ferment for 5 to 6 weeks.

13. Once the fermentation has stopped, carefully pour the liquid into wine bottles that have been sterilized, making sure not to disturb the sediment. (Leave the sediment in the bottom of the container.)

14. Cork or cap the wine bottles. Let the wine stand for 1 year before drinking.

Spiced Mulled Wine or "Pink Tea"

Kuhano Vino

On Christmas Eve, the head of the Slovenian family walks through the house and the farmstead with all following, to bless every corner of the house, the barns, and the livestock with holy water and incense. The family then prays together for a rich and bountiful year ahead. They head to church for midnight mass, and, upon returning home, warm themselves with a cup of spiced mulled wine, called "pink tea." An old legend says that on Christmas Eve the livestock are able to speak, since the animals were the only ones to witness Jesus Christ's birth. However, only the pure of heart and mind are able to hear them.

Serves 12

**4 bottles dark red wine,
   such as a burgundy**
2 cinnamon sticks
5 or 6 whole cloves
1 teaspoon allspice berries
**1 to 1½ cups sugar, as
   desired**
½ lemon, sliced
½ orange, sliced

1. Combine all ingredients in a large saucepan.
2. Cook over medium to high heat, stirring occasionally. Continue to cook for 20 to 25 minutes, or until all flavors are combined.
3. Serve hot with cookies, cake or potica.

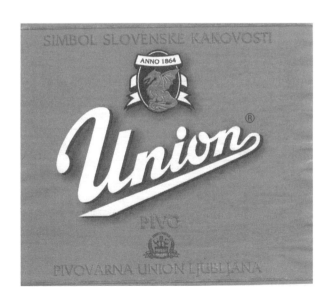

The logo for the wine labels from the Simčič vineyards in Goriška.

The Union Beer label from the Union
Brewery in Ljubljana.

Blueberry Liqueur Borovnični Liker

You may use wild or cultivated berries to make this sweet and tasty blueberry brandy.

Makes 2 to 3 small bottles of brandy

4 cups blueberries (preferably fresh, but you may also use frozen)
1 cup water, boiled and allowed to cool
3 cups sugar
5 or 6 whole cloves
1 vanilla bean
1 stick cinnamon
4 cups plain brandy, preferably plum or vodka

1. Place the blueberries in a large pan and cover with the water. Allow to sit, covered, for 1 day.

2. Press the mixture through a cheesecloth, reserving the liquid. Save some of the pressed berries.

3. In a medium saucepan, place the sugar and 2 cups of water. Cook over high heat, stirring continuously, until the mixture boils. Remove from heat and allow to cool.

4. Pour the sugar water into the blueberry juice, through a strainer.

5. Add the spices and the brandy to the blueberry juice. Add some of the pressed blueberries for color.

6. Pour the mixture into clean bottles, which you can seal loosely.

7. Allow the bottles to stand in the sun for several days, turning them occasionally.

8. Pour the liqueur into sterilized bottles and seal tightly. It may be drunk immediately!

Walnut Liqueur Orehov Liker

15 walnuts, shelled and
  sliced
4 cups brandy, preferably
  plum or vodka
12 raisins or currants
  (optional)
Zest from 2 oranges
½ vanilla bean
2 cups sugar
1 cup water

1. In a large bottle, combine the walnuts and the brandy. Add raisins or currants, if you are using them.

2. Cover loosely and allow to sit in the sun for up to 10 days.

3. Pour the liquid through a strainer into a bottle and add the orange peel and the vanilla bean.

4. Close the bottle and allow to sit in the sun for 4 days. Shake the bottle occasionally.

5. Pour the liquid into a large saucepan and add the sugar and water. Cook over medium heat, stirring continuously for 15 to 20 minutes. Skim off any foam that rises to the surface.

6. Remove from heat and allow to cool.

7. Pour into sterilized bottles and seal tightly. The walnut liqueur is ready to drink immediately!

Nihèe ne ljubi domovine, ker je velika, temveè ker je njegova.
Nobody loves their homeland because it's great, but because it's theirs.

– Slovenian proverb

BIBLIOGRAPHY

Art Nouveau Ljubljana, brochure printed by the Ljubljana Tourist Information Center, Ljubljana, Slovenia.

Black Lamb and Grey Falcon, A Journey through Yugoslavia, by Rebecca West, Canongate Classics, Edinburgh, Scotland, 1997.

Bled, promotional materials printed by the Bled Tourist Office, Bled, Slovenia.

Bled Thousand Years, by Jože Dežman, Didakta Radovljica, Radovljica, Slovenia, 2004.

Classic Italian Cookbook, The, Julia Della Croce, published by Dorling Kindersley, London, England, 1996.

Croatia at Table, The Aromas and Tastes of Croatian Cuisine, by Ivanka Biluš, Božica Brkan, Lidija Ćorić, and Cirila Rodè, Alfa d.d., Zagreb, Croatia, 1997.

Croatian Cuisine, The Modern Way, by Ivanka Biluš, Lidija Ćorić, Zdenka Kocmur, Cirila Rodè, and Ljiljana Šprem, Golden Marketing, Zagreb, Croatia, 1995.

France Prešeren Poems, selected and edited by France Pibernik and Franc Drolc, translated into English by Tom M. S. Priestly and Henry R. Cooper, Jr., published by the Municipality of Kranj, Slovenia, printed by Gorenjski tisk, Kranj, Slovenia, 2001.

Gundel's Hungarian Cookbook, translated by Ágnes Kádár, published by the estate of Károly Gundel, printed by Sylvester János Printing House, Szombathely, Hungary, 2001.

Hungarian Cuisine, translated by Gabriella Molnár, published by The Heirs of Mariska Vizvári, printed by DTP Impala House, Szeged, Hungary, 1994.

Hungarian Cuisine, written and edited by György and Csaba Hunyaddobrai, translated by Zsuzsanna Gáspár, published by Média Nova, printed by Dürer Nyomda, Gyula, Hungary, 2001.

Kuhinja Slovenije, Mojstrovine Nove Kuharske Umetnosti, by Janez Bogataj, Juluj Nemanič and Slavko Adamlje, published by Založba Rokus, d.o.o., Ljubljana, Slovenia, 2000.

More Pots and Pans, A Cookbook of the Slovenian Women's Union of America, compiled by National Officers Slovenian Women's Union of America, printed by the Croatian Franciscan Press, Chicago, IL, 1998.

Museum of Apiculture in Radovljica, The, promotional material printed by the Beekeeping Museum, Radovljica, Slovenia.

New German Cookbook, The, by Jean Anderson and Hedy Würz, Harper Collins, New York, NY 1993.

Slovene, English – Slovene, Slovene – English Modern Dictionary, Daša Komac, Hippocrene Books, Inc., New York, NY, 1998.

Slovenia, Europe in Miniature, by Neil Wilson and Steve Fallon, Lonely Planet Publications, Melbourne, Australia, 2001.

Slovenian Cookery, Over 100 Classic Dishes, edited by Tatjana Žener, published by Mladinska knjiga, Ljubljana, Slovenia, 1996.

Slovenian Cooking, text by Andrej Fritz, translated by Simona Pečnik-Kržič, published by Turistika, Golnik, Slovenia, 2001.

Slovene Proverbs and Sayings, selected by Marjeta Zorec, edited by Andreja Peček, published by Mladinska knjiga, Ljubljana, Slovenia, 2001.

Sundays at Moosewood Restaurant, Ethnic and Regional Recipes from the Cooks at Moosewood Restaurant, Simon and Schuster/Fireside, New York, NY, 1990.

INDEX

SIDEBAR INDEX

Cuisines of the Alps: Recipes, Drinks, and Lore from France, Switzerland, Liechtenstein, Italy, Germany, Austria, and Slovenia
Kay Shaw Nelson

A majestic mountain system in south-central Europe, the Alps form an arc spanning almost 750 miles from the Mediterranean Sea through northern Italy and southeast France, Switzerland, southern Germany, and Austria and into the northwest part of the Balkan Peninsula. *Cuisines of the Alps* takes a culinary tour through this region with stops in Northern Italy for risotto a la Milanese and osso buco; in Austrian for goulash and linzer torte; for dumplings in Bavaria; *raclette* in Switzerland; French *trout au bleu*, and in Slovenia for eggplant stew and walnut cake. *Cuisines of the Alps* will enhance your knowledge of the region's cookery, bringing the snow-capped peaks, with their robust, homey dishes into your kitchen.

197 pages • 6 x 9 • 2-color • 0-7818-1058-2 • $24.95hc • (59)

The Best of Croatian Cooking, Expanded Edition
Liliana Pavicic & Gordana Pirker-Mosher

Croatia, a beautiful and geographically diverse country on Europe's Balkan peninsula, offers a sunny Adriatic coastline and breathtaking scenery, as well as a distinctive culinary tradition that combines central European, Mediterranean, and Near Eastern influences.

The more than 200 recipes feature classic dishes like Turkey with Pasta Tatters, Strudel with Sautéed Cabbage, and Black Risotto, which is prepared with cuttlefish ink. Also included are over 50 dessert recipes for fine tortes, cookies, and all variety of strudels (poppy seed, carob, apple, apricot, cheese, walnut and more). The authors' introduction to Croatia and its cuisine provides insight into the development of the culinary tradition through the centuries, as well as the specialties of the various regions in Croatia. The addition of a chapter on Croatian wines completes the culinary tour offered through the pages of this book.

Also included are time-saving tips and ideas for lightening the recipes to accommodate modern tastes and healthy lifestyles. The recipes are in a step-by-step format, and all are adapted for the North American kitchen.

311 pages • 6 x 9 • ISBN 13: 978-0-7818-1203-0 • ISBN 10: 0-7818-1203-0 • $16.95pb • (220)

Hungarian Cookbook: Old World Recipes for New World Cooks
Expanded Edition
Yolanda Nagy Fintor

These Old World recipes were brought to America by the author's grandparents, but they have been updated to accommodate today's faster-paced lifestyles. In many cases, the author presents a New World version of the recipe, in which low-fat and more readily available ingredients are substituted without compromising flavor. This collection includes timeless dishes, and spans the range of home cooking with recipes for Kohlrabi Soup, Stuffed Cabbage, Chicken Paprika, and a host of tempting desserts like Walnut Torte and Dilled Cottage Cheese Cake. The new chapter on breads focuses on yeast breads, with a short section on quick breads. It includes recipes for Sour Cream Biscuits, Hungarian Fried Bread, and Beer Bread Sticks, among others.

This is more than just a collection of 142 enticing Hungarian recipes. The author offers culinary tips, explains characteristics of the Hungarian language, and includes a glossary of terms used throughout the book. Several chapters also describe the seasonal and ceremonial observances transplanted from Hungary and still practiced by Americans of Hungarian descent: bacon cookouts, Fall grape festivals, weddings, baptisms, Christmas, New Year's, and Easter celebrations.

216 pages • 5½ x 8½ • 0-7818-0996-7 • $24.95hc • (382)

Best of Austrian Cuisine, Expanded Edition
Elisabeth Mayer-Browne

Austrian cuisine consists of rich, satisfying dishes: roasted meats in cream sauces, hearty soups and stews, tasty dumplings, warm and cold salads, and, of course, the pastries and cakes that remain Vienna's trademark. This cookbook provides a comprehensive guide to Austrian desserts, including six recipes for strudel, twenty recipes for gateaux, and many other sweet-tooth favorites. A new guide to Austrian wines provides the history, main varieties, and regional information about the Austrian winemaking tradition.

Elisabeth Mayer-Browne takes an engaging, conversational approach to her art with commonsense advice about preparing, serving, and even improvising. *The Best of Austrian Cuisine* includes nearly 200 recipes for traditional family favorites, interesting variations, and menus for everyday meals and holidays.

224 pages • 5½ x 8½ • 0-7818-0526-0 • $11.95pb • (633)

Cucina di Calabria
Mary Amabile Palmer

Nearly 200 recipes offer something for every cook, whether novice or experienced. All start with simple, fresh ingredients, transformed into sumptuous dishes with a minimum of effort. They are interwoven with anecdotes about Calabrian culture and history, traditions, festivals, folklore, and of course, the primary role that food plays in all aspects of Italian life.

For centuries, Calabrian food has remained relatively undiscovered because few recipes were divulged beyond tightly knit villages or even family circles, but Mary Amabile Palmer has gathered a comprehensive collection of exciting, robust recipes from the home of her ancestors. *Cucina di Calabria* is a celebration of the adventurous and creative cuisine she knows intimately and loves.

320 pages • 7½ x 10 • 0-7818-1050-7 • $18.95pb • (660)

A Ligurian Kitchen
Recipes and Tales from the Italian Riviera
Laura Giannatempo

The Ligurian kitchen is famous for fish, fresh produce and herbs. Dishes like *Maltagliati con Pesto Piccantino* (Fresh Maltagliati with Spicy Purple Pesto) and *Ciuppin con Crostoni di Paprika* (Ligurian Seafood Bisque with Paprika Crostoni) are featured along with such quintessential favorites as *Orata al Forno con Olive Nere e Patatine Arrosto* (Roasted Orata with Black Olives and Baby Potatoes). But tales of lovable uncles and a lyrical account of making pasta in the midst of a storm tantalize as much as these sumptuous repasts. In these 100 recipes and a beautiful section of photographs, the specialties of artisanal bread bakers and those of the region's *cucina povera* to create a zestful collection that exemplifies "that extraordinary marriage of land and sea that is Ligurian cuisine."

200 pages • 9 x 8 • two-color • 16 page color insert • 0-7818-1171-6 • $29.00hc • (8)

Sicilian Feasts
Giovanna Bellia La Marca

Sicilian Feasts was born out of the author's love of her native Sicily. She shares the history, customs, and folklore, as well as the flavorful and varied cuisines of her beautiful Mediterranean island in recipes, stories and anecdotes. Sicilian Feasts offers more than 160 recipes, along with menus for holidays, notes on ingredients, list of supplies, an introduction to the Sicilian language, and a glossary of food terms in Sicilian, Italian, and English. Illustrations demonstrate special techniques.

220 pages • 6 x 9 • two-color • 0-7818-0967-3 • $24.95hc • (539)

A Treasury of Italian Cuisine (Bilingual)
Recipes, Sayings and Proverbs in Italian and English
Joseph F. Privitera

Learn the basics of hearty and delicious Italian cooking in this appealing bilingual cookbook. Among the 60 recipes in Italian and English are such staples as *Cozze alla Parmigiana* (Baked Mussels), *Minestrone, Salsa di Pomodoro* (Basic Tomato Sauce), *Ossobuco al Marsala* (Veal Shanks in Marsala), and *Cannoli Siciliani* (Sicilian Cannoli), all adapted for the modern cook and the North American kitchen. Line drawings, proverbs and bits of folk wisdom add to the volume's charm. This book is the perfect gift for students of the Italian culinary tradition, culture and language.

146 pages • 5 x 7 • line drawings • 0-7818-0740-9 • $11.95hc • (149)

Prices subject to change without prior notice.

To purchase Hippocrene Books contact your local bookstore, call (718) 454-2366, or write to: HIPPOCRENE BOOKS, 171 Madison Avenue, New York, NY 10016. Please enclose check or money order, adding $5.00 shipping (UPS) for the first book, and $.50 for each additional book.